C000162739

The confessions of J. J. Rousseau: with the reveries of the solitary walker. Translated from the French. ... Volume 1 of 2

Jean-Jacques Rousseau

ECCO
PRINT EDITIONS

The confessions of J. J. Rousseau: with the reveries of the solitary walker. Translated from the French. ... Volume 1 of 2
Rousseau, Jean-Jacques
ESTCID: T136470
Reproduction from British Library

London : printed for J. Bew, 1783.
2v. ; 12°

Eighteenth Century
Collections Online
Print Editions

Gale ECCO Print Editions

Relive history with *Eighteenth Century Collections Online*, now available in print for the independent historian and collector. This series includes the most significant English-language and foreign-language works printed in Great Britain during the eighteenth century, and is organized in seven different subject areas including literature and language; medicine, science, and technology; and religion and philosophy. The collection also includes thousands of important works from the Americas.

The eighteenth century has been called "The Age of Enlightenment." It was a period of rapid advance in print culture and publishing, in world exploration, and in the rapid growth of science and technology – all of which had a profound impact on the political and cultural landscape. At the end of the century the American Revolution, French Revolution and Industrial Revolution, perhaps three of the most significant events in modern history, set in motion developments that eventually dominated world political, economic, and social life.

In a groundbreaking effort, Gale initiated a revolution of its own: digitization of epic proportions to preserve these invaluable works in the largest online archive of its kind. Contributions from major world libraries constitute over 175,000 original printed works. Scanned images of the actual pages, rather than transcriptions, recreate the works *as they first appeared.*

Now for the first time, these high-quality digital scans of original works are available via print-on-demand, making them readily accessible to libraries, students, independent scholars, and readers of all ages.

For our initial release we have created seven robust collections to form one the world's most comprehensive catalogs of 18th century works.

Initial Gale ECCO Print Editions collections include:

History and Geography
Rich in titles on English life and social history, this collection spans the world as it was known to eighteenth-century historians and explorers. Titles include a wealth of travel accounts and diaries, histories of nations from throughout the world, and maps and charts of a world that was still being discovered. Students of the War of American Independence will find fascinating accounts from the British side of conflict.

Social Science

Delve into what it was like to live during the eighteenth century by reading the first-hand accounts of everyday people, including city dwellers and farmers, businessmen and bankers, artisans and merchants, artists and their patrons, politicians and their constituents. Original texts make the American, French, and Industrial revolutions vividly contemporary.

Medicine, Science and Technology

Medical theory and practice of the 1700s developed rapidly, as is evidenced by the extensive collection, which includes descriptions of diseases, their conditions, and treatments. Books on science and technology, agriculture, military technology, natural philosophy, even cookbooks, are all contained here.

Literature and Language

Western literary study flows out of eighteenth-century works by Alexander Pope, Daniel Defoe, Henry Fielding, Frances Burney, Denis Diderot, Johann Gottfried Herder, Johann Wolfgang von Goethe, and others. Experience the birth of the modern novel, or compare the development of language using dictionaries and grammar discourses.

Religion and Philosophy

The Age of Enlightenment profoundly enriched religious and philosophical understanding and continues to influence present-day thinking. Works collected here include masterpieces by David Hume, Immanuel Kant, and Jean-Jacques Rousseau, as well as religious sermons and moral debates on the issues of the day, such as the slave trade. The Age of Reason saw conflict between Protestantism and Catholicism transformed into one between faith and logic -- a debate that continues in the twenty-first century.

Law and Reference

This collection reveals the history of English common law and Empire law in a vastly changing world of British expansion. Dominating the legal field is the *Commentaries of the Law of England* by Sir William Blackstone, which first appeared in 1765. Reference works such as almanacs and catalogues continue to educate us by revealing the day-to-day workings of society.

Fine Arts

The eighteenth-century fascination with Greek and Roman antiquity followed the systematic excavation of the ruins at Pompeii and Herculaneum in southern Italy; and after 1750 a neoclassical style dominated all artistic fields. The titles here trace developments in mostly English-language works on painting, sculpture, architecture, music, theater, and other disciplines. Instructional works on musical instruments, catalogs of art objects, comic operas, and more are also included.

The BiblioLife Network

This project was made possible in part by the BiblioLife Network (BLN), a project aimed at addressing some of the huge challenges facing book preservationists around the world. The BLN includes libraries, library networks, archives, subject matter experts, online communities and library service providers. We believe every book ever published should be available as a high-quality print reproduction; printed on-demand anywhere in the world. This insures the ongoing accessibility of the content and helps generate sustainable revenue for the libraries and organizations that work to preserve these important materials.

The following book is in the "public domain" and represents an authentic reproduction of the text as printed by the original publisher. While we have attempted to accurately maintain the integrity of the original work, there are sometimes problems with the original work or the micro-film from which the books were digitized. This can result in minor errors in reproduction. Possible imperfections include missing and blurred pages, poor pictures, markings and other reproduction issues beyond our control. Because this work is culturally important, we have made it available as part of our commitment to protecting, preserving, and promoting the world's literature.

GUIDE TO FOLD-OUTS MAPS and OVERSIZED IMAGES

The book you are reading was digitized from microfilm captured over the past thirty to forty years. Years after the creation of the original microfilm, the book was converted to digital files and made available in an online database.

In an online database, page images do not need to conform to the size restrictions found in a printed book. When converting these images back into a printed bound book, the page sizes are standardized in ways that maintain the detail of the original. For large images, such as fold-out maps, the original page image is split into two or more pages

Guidelines used to determine how to split the page image follows:

• Some images are split vertically; large images require vertical and horizontal splits.
• For horizontal splits, the content is split left to right.
• For vertical splits, the content is split from top to bottom.
• For both vertical and horizontal splits, the image is processed from top left to bottom right.

THE
CONFESSIONS

OF

J. J. ROUSSEAU:

WITH THE

REVERIES

OF THE

SOLITARY WALKER.

TRANSLATED FROM THE FRENCH.

VOL. I.

LONDON:

Printed for J. Bew, in Pater-Noster-Row.

MDCCLXXXIII.

THE
CONFESSIONS

OF

J. J. ROUSSEAU.

BOOK I.

I AM undertaking a work which has no example, and whose execution will have no imitator. I mean to lay open to my fellow-mortals a man juft as nature wrought him, and this man is myfelf.

I alone. I know my heart, and am acquainted with mankind. I am not made like any one I have feen; I dare believe I am not made like any one exifting. If I am not better, at leaft I am quite different. Whether Nature has done well or ill in breaking the mould fhe caft me in, can be determined only after having read me.

Let the trumpet of the day of judgment found when it will, I fhall appear with this book in my hand before the Sovereign Judge, and cry with a loud voice, This is my work, thefe were my thoughts, and thus was I. I have freely told both the good and the bad, have hid nothing wicked, added nothing good; and if I have happened to make ufe of an

VOL. I.   B   infig-

infignificant ornament, 'twas only to fill a void occafioned by a fhort memory: I may have fuppofed true what I knew might be fo, never what I knew was falfe. I have expofed myfelf as I was, contemptible and vile fome times; at others, good, generous, and fublime. I have revealed my heart as thou faweft it thyfelf. Eternal Being! affemble around me the numberlefs throng of my fellow-mortals; let them liften to my Confeffions, let them lament at my unworthinefs, let them blufh at my mifery. Let each of them, in his turn, lay open his heart with the fame fincerity at the foot of thy throne, and then fay, if he dare, *I was better than that man.*

I was born at Geneva in 1712, of Ifaac Roufleau, and Sufan Bernard, citizens. A very moderate eftate, which was divided amongft fifteen children, having reduced almoft to nothing my father's fhare, he had no other fubfiftance than his trade, which was that of a watchmaker, in which he was undoubtedly very clever. My mother, a daughter of the minifter Bernard, was richer; fhe had prudence and beauty: 'twas with fome trouble my father obtained her. Their affection began almoft at their birth. from the age of eight or nine they took a walk together every evening on the banks of the Treille; at the age of ten they could never leave each other. Sympathy and refemblance of foul ftrengthened in them the fentiments habit had produced. Each born for tendernefs and fenfibility, only waited for the moment to find another of the fame difpofition, or rather that moment

moment waited for them, and each of them gave their heart to the first expanded to receive it. Fate, which seemed to oppose their passion, animated it still more The young lover, not able to obtain his beloved, wasted away with sorrow; she advised him to travel and forget her. He travelled in vain, and returned more fond than ever. He found her again whom he loved, tender and faithful. After this proof nothing remained but to love each other for life; they vowed it, and Heaven blessed their vow.

Gabriel Bernard, my mother's brother, fell in love with one of the sisters of my father; but she would not consent to marry the brother on any condition but that of her brother's marrying the sister. Love arranged all, and the two marriages were celebrated the same day. Thus my uncle married my aunt, and their children were doubly my cousin-germans. Each of them had a child before the end of the year; and once more they were obliged to separate.

My Uncle Bernard was an engineer: he served in the Empire and in Hungary under prince Eugene. He distinguished himself at the siege and battle of Belgrade My father, after the birth of my only brother, set off for Constantinople, by desire, and became watchmaker to the Seraglio During his absence, the beauty of my mother, her wit, and talents *, drew admirers. M. de la Closure, resident

* They were too brilliant for her situation; the minister her father, who adored her, having taken

dent of France, was the forwardeſt in his
effers His paſſion muſt have been intenſe , for
thirty years afterwards I have ſeen him melt
at her name My mother had more than
common virtue for her defence · ſhe tenderly
loved her huſband ; ſhe preſſed him to return.
He left all and came I was the unhappy
fruit of this return. Ten months after I
came into the world infirm and ill ; I coſt my
mother her life, and my birth was the firſt of
my misfortunes.

I don't know how my father ſupported this
loſs , but I know he was never happy afterwards He thought he ſaw her in me, without being able to forget I had taken her from
him never did he claſp me in his arms, but I
felt, by his ſighs, by his convulſive embraces,
that a bitter regret was mixt with his careſſes,
though they were the tenderer for it Whenever he ſaid to me, Jean Jacques, let us talk
of thy mother, I ſaid, Well, father, we ſhall
cry then , and this word alone immediately drew

great care of her education. She was taught
drawing and ſinging, ſhe accompanied the the-
orbo, had learning, and compoſed tolerable verſe.
Here is an extempory piece of hers, in the abſence
of her brother and huſband, while walking with
her ſiſter-in-law and their two children, on a converſation with ſome one about them.

Ces deux Meſſieurs, qui font abſens,
Nous font chers de bien des manieres ;
Ce font nos amis, nos amans ;
Ce font nos maris & nos freres,
Et les peres de ces enfans.

tears

tears from him.   Ah! faid he with a groan, give her back to me again; comfort me for her; fill up the fpace fhe has left in my foul. Could I love thee thus, if thou waft only mine? Forty years after her death, he died in the arms of a fecond wife; but the name of the firft was on his tongue, and her image in his heart.

Such were the authors of my being.   Of all the gifts heaven had beftowed on them, a feeling heart was the only one they left me; but that which was their happinefs, caufed all the misfortunes of my life.

I came into the world almoft dead; they had little hopes of preferving me.   I brought with me the feeds of a diforder which years have ftrengthened, and which now I am fome-times relieved from, only to fuffer otherwife in a more cruel manner.   A fifter of my father, an amiable and prudent young woman, took fo much care of me that fhe faved me.   At the time I write this, fhe is ftill living, nurfing at eighty a hufband younger than herfelf, but worn out by excefs in drinking.   Dear aunt, I excufe you for having faved my life, and am forry I cannot return you, at the decline of your days, thofe tender cares you heaped on me at the beginning of mine.   I have likewife my governefs Jaqueline ftill alive, healthy and robuft.   The hands, which opened my eyes at my birth, may clofe them at my death.

I felt before I thought; 'tis the common fate of humanity: I have proved it more than any one.   I am ignorant of what paffed till I was five or fix years old: I don't know how I

learnt

learnt to read; I remember my firft ftudies only, and their effect on me : this is the time from whence I date, without interruption, the knowledge of myfelf. My mother left fome romances My father and I read them after fupper. At that time the point was to exercife me in reading entertaining books only, but very foon the intereft in them became fo ftrong, that we read by turns without ceafing, and paffed whole nights at this employment. We never could leave off but at the end of the volume. Sometimes my father, on hearing the fwallows in the morning, would fay, quite afhamed, Come, let us go to bed; I am more a child than thou art.

In a fhort time I acquired, by this dangerous method, not only an extreme facility in reading and comprehending, but alfo a peculiar knowledge at my age of the paffions. I had not the leaft idea of things, but the fentiments were known to me. I conceived nothing; I had felt the whole. Thefe confufed emotions, which I found come one on the other, did not hurt the reafon I was not yet poffeffed of; but they formed one of another fort, and gave me a romantic extravagant notion of human life, which experience and reflection have never been able entirely to eradicate.

The romances ended with the fummer of 1719. The winter following produced other things. My mother's library being exhaufted, recourfe was had to that part of her father's which had fallen to our fhare. Happily we found fome good books among them it could not well be otherwife, this library having
been

been collected by a minifter in the true fenfe
of the word, and not only learned, (for it was
then the fafhion,) but alfo a man of tafte and
fenfe.   The Hiftory of the Church and of the
Empire by Le Sueur, the Difcourfes of Boffuet
on Univerfal Hiftory, Plutarch's Illuftrious
Men, the Hiftory of Venice by Nani, Ovid's
Metamorphofes, La Bruyere, Fontenelle's
Worlds, his Dialogues of the Dead, and a few
volumes of Moliere, were carried to my father's
clofet, and I read them to him every day during
his employment.   My tafte for them was uncommon, and perhaps not to be equalled at
that age.   Plutarch, particularly, became my
favourite author.   The pleafure I took in reading him over again and again, cured me a little
of romances, and I foon preferred Agefilaus,
Brutus, and Ariftides, to Orondates, Arta-
menes, and Juba.   From thefe engaging
ftudies, from the converfations they occafioned
between my father and me, were formed that
liberal republican fpirit, that proud invincible
character, impatient of reftraint or fervitude,
which has tortured me through the whole
courfe of my life, in fituations the leaft proper
for giving them action.   Inceffantly occupied
with Rome or Athens, living in a manner with
their great men, myfelf born citizen of a
republic, and fon to a father whofe love of his
country was his ruling paffion, I glowed at
his example; I thought myfelf Greek or Roman, I was transformed into the perfon whofe
life I read. the recital of an act of conftancy
and intrepidity which ftruck me, rendered my
eyes fiery, and my voice ftrong.   One day at

table, reciting the ftory of Scævola, they were affrighted to fee me go forward, and hold my hand over a chafing-difh, to reprefent his action.

I had a brother feven years older than me. He learned the profeffion of my father. The extreme affection for me caufed him to be a little neglected, and this is not what I approve of. His education felt this negligence. He gave into libertinifm, even before the age of a real libertine. He was fent to another mafter, where he played the fame pranks as at home. I feldom faw him, I can fcarcely fay I was acquainted with him; but I neverthelefs loved him tenderly, and he loved me as much as a rake can love any body. I recollect once, when my father chaftized him feverely and in anger, I threw myfelf impetuoufly between them, and clofely embraced him. I covered him thus with my body, receiving the ftrokes aimed at him. I perfifted fo much in this attitude, that my father was at laft obliged to pardon him, either foftened by my cries and tears, or being unwilling to beat me more than him. In fine, my brother grew fo bad, he went off, and entirely difappeared. Some time after we heard he was in Germany. He never once wrote. He has never fince been heard of, and thus I became the only fon.

Though the poor boy was neglected, it was not fo with his brother; the fons of kings could not be better taken care of than I was during my tender years by all around me, and always, which is very rare, treated as a beloved, not as a fpoiled child: not once, whilft under

paternal

paternal infpection, was I permitted to run about the ftreets with other children; never required reprimand or gratification in any fantaftical humour, imputed to nature, but which fprings from education only. I had the faults of my age; I was a prattler, a glutton, and fometimes a liar. I fometimes ftole fruit, fweetmeats, and victuals; but I never took pleafure in mifchief, wafte, accufing others, or torturing poor animals. I remember, however, making water once in the kettle of one of our neighbours, whofe name was madam Clot, while fhe was at church. I own too the recollection ftill makes me laugh, becaufe madam Clot, a good creature if you pleafe, was, however, the moft grumbling old woman I ever knew. Thus you have the fhort and true hiftory of all my childifh mifdeeds.

How could I become wicked, when I had nothing before my eyes but examples of mild-nefs, and around me the beft people in the world? My father, my aunt, my governefs, my relations, my acquaintance, my neighbours, all who furrounded me, did not obey me indeed, but loved me, and I on my part loved them. My wifhes were fo little excited and fo little contradicted, I never thought of any. I can make oath that until my fubjection to a mafter, I never knew what a caprice was. Except the time I fpent in reading, or writing with my father, or that my governefs took me out a walking; I was always with my aunt, ob-ferving her embroider, hearing her fing, fitting or ftanding by her fide, and I was happy. Her

fprightlinefs, her mildnefs, her agreeable countenance, are fo ftrongly imprinted on me, that
I yet fee her manner, her looks, her attitude;
I remember her little carefling queftions; I
could tell her cloathing and head-drefs, without
forgetting the two locks her black hair formed
on her, temples, according to the fafhion of
thofe times.

I am perfuaded I am indebted to her for a
tafte, or rather paffion, for mufic, which did not
fhew itfelf till long afterwards. She knew a
prodigious number of tunes and fongs, which
fhe fung with a foft and melodious voice.
The ferenity of foul of this excellent girl drove
from her, and thofe who furrounded her, fadnefs
and melancholy. The charms of her voice fo
allured me, that not only feveral of her fongs
remain in my memory, but fome of them come
to my recollection, now I have loft her, though
totally forgot fince my infancy, and prefent
themfelves ftill as I grow old, with a charm
I am not able to exprefs. Would one think
that I, an old dotard, worn out with care and
-trouble, furprize myfelf fometimes in tears
like a child, in muttering thefe little tunes with
a voice already broke and trembling? One
of them in particular I have recollected entirely again, as to the tune; but the fecond
moiety of the words conftantly refufes every
effort to recal it, though I catch the rhimes in
a confufed manner of fome of them. Here is
the beginning, and what I have been able to
recollect of the remainder.

Tircis,

Tircis, je n'ose
Ecouter ton chalumeau
Sous l' ormeau ;
Car on en cause
Déjà dans notre hameau.
. . . .
. . . . un berger
. . . . s'engager
. . . . sans danger ;
Et toûjours l' épine est sous la rose.

I have sought for the moving charm my
heart feels at this song · 'tis a caprice I cannot
comprehend ; but there is an impossibility of
my singing it to the end without being suffo-
cated by tears. I have an hundred times
intended to write to Paris, to get the remaining
words, if it should happen that any one still
knows them. But I am almost sure the pleasure I take in recalling them to my mind would
vanish in part, if I had a proof that any other
than my poor aunt Susan sung them.

Such were the first affections of my entrance
into life, thus was formed and began to shew
itself that heart of mine at once so proud and
so tender, that character so effeminate, but
nevertheless invincible, which, always floating
between weakness and courage, between ease
and virtue, has even to the last set me in contradiction with myself, and has caused abstin-
ence and enjoyment, pleasure and prudence,
equally to shun me.

This course of education was interrupted
by an accident whose consequences influenced
the rest of my life. My father had a dispute

with

with a Mr. G***, a captain in France, and related to some of the council. This G***, an insolent and ungenerous man, bled at the nose, and to revenge himself accused my father of having drawn his sword against him in the city. My father, whom they wanted to send to prison, insisted that, according to law, the accuser should be sent there likewise Not being able to obtain it, he chose rather to leave Geneva and quit his country for the rest of his life, than to give up a point where honour and liberty seemed in danger.

I remained under the tuition of my uncle Bernard, at that time employed in the fortifications of Geneva. His eldest daughter was dead, but he had a son about my age. We were both sent to board at Bossey with the minister Lambercier, to learn, with Latin, all the insignificant stuff which accompanies it, under the name of education.

Two years spent in a village softened a little my Roman fierceness, and brought me back to my state of childhood. At Geneva, where nothing was forced on me, I was fond of application and study; 'twas almost my whole amusement. At Bossey application made me fond of play as a relaxation. The country was so new to me 'twas impossible to tire myself with its enjoyment. My taste for it was a passion I never could extinguish. The remembrance of the happy days I have passed in it, makes me regret its abode and its pleasures at every age, quite to that which has brought me there again. M. Lambercier was a very sensible man, who, without neglecting our in-
                                        struction,

ſtruction, never loaded us with extreme taſks. The proof his method was a good one is, that, in ſpite of my averſion to conſtraint, I never recollect with diſguſt my hours of ſtudy; and though I did not learn much of him, what I learnt was without trouble, and I ſtill retain it.

The ſimplicity of that rural life was an advantage ineſtimable, as it opened my heart to friendſhip. Till then I had been acquainted with elevated, but imaginary ſentiments only. The habit of living in a peaceable ſtate together tenderly united me to my couſin Bernard. In a little time i had more affectionate ſentiments for him, than thoſe I had for my brother, and which have never worn away. He was a tall, long-ſhanked, weakly boy, with a mind as mild as his body was feeble, and did not much abuſe the partiality ſhewn him in the houſe as ſon of my guardian. Our labour, our amuſements, our taſtes, were the ſame; we were alone, of the ſame age; each of us wanted a play-mate: to ſeparate us was in ſome meaſure to annihilate us. Though we had not many opportunities of ſhewing our attachment to each other, it was extreme; and not only we could not live an inſtant ſeparated, but we even thought we never could endure it. Each of a humour to yield to kindneſs, complaiſant if not conſtrained, we always agreed on every point. If, favoured by thoſe who governed us, he had the aſcendant over me while in their ſight, when we were alone I had it over him, which eſtabliſhed the equilibrium. At our ſtudies, I prompted him

1f

if he hefitated; when my exercife was done I helped him in doing his, and at our amufements my more active tafte always guided him. In fine, our two characters were fo alike, and the friendfhip which united us fo real, that for more than five years that we were nearly infeparable, both at Boffey and Geneva, we often fought, I allow, but it was never neceffary to feparate us; no one of our difputes lafted more than a quarter of an hour, and we never once accufed each other. Thefe remarks are, if you will, puerile; but the refult is, perhaps, a fingular example fince children have exifted.

The manner I lived in at Boffey was fo agreeable, that nothing but its continuance was neceffary abfolutely to fix my character. Tender, affectionate, peaceable fentiments were its bafis. I believe an individual of our fpecies never had naturally lefs vanity than I. I raifed myfelf by tranfports to fublime emotions, but as fuddenly I returned to my languor. To be loved by all who faw me was my greateft wifh. I was mild, fo was my coufin, thofe who governed us were the fame. During two years I was neither witnefs nor victim of a violent fentiment. Every thing nourifhed in my heart the difpofitions it received from nature: I knew nothing fo chaiming as to fee every one contented with me and every thing elfe. I fhall for ever remember, that, at church, anfwering our catechifm, nothing fo much troubled me, when I happened to hefitate, as to fee, in the countenance of Mifs Lambercier, marks of uneafinefs and trouble.

trouble. That alone afflicted me more than the shame of faultering in public, which, however, extremely affected me: for, though not very sensible to praise, I always was very much to shame; and I can now say, that the expectation of a reprimand from Miss Lambercier alarmed me less than the dread of making her uneasy.

However, she did not, on occasion, want severity any more than her brother; but as this severity, almost always just, was never in anger, it afflicted me, but without complaining. I was more sorry to displease than to be punished, and the sign of discontent was more cruel to me than afflictive correction. It is painful to me, but I must speak plainer. The method taken with youth would be changed, if the distant effects were better seen, from what is always indiscriminately, and often indiscretely, made use of. The great lesson to be learnt from an example as common as fatal, made me resolve to give it.

As Miss Lambercier had a mother's affection for us, she had also the authority, and sometimes carried it so far as to inflict on us the punishment of infants, when we deserved it. She confined herself long enough to menaces, and menaces were so new to me as to seem very dreadful; but after their execution, I found them less terrible in the proof than in the expectation, and, what is more extraordinary, the chastisement drew my affection still more towards her who gave it. Nothing less than the reality of this affection, and all my natural mildness, could have prevented me me from feeing a return of the fame treatment in deferving it; for I felt in my grief, and even in my fhame, a mixture of fenfuality which left more defire than fear to experience it again from the fame hand. It is certain, that, as there was, without doubt, a forward inftinct of the fex in it, the fame chaftifement from her brother would not have appeared in the leaft pleafing But from a man of his humour this fubftitution was not much to be feared, and if I did abftain from meriting correction, it was only for fear of vexing Mifs Lambercier: for fuch an empire has benevolence eftablifhed in me, and even that the fenfes have given birth to, they always give law to my heart.

This relapfe, which I retarded without dreading, happened without my fault, that is my will, and I benefited by it, I may fay with a fafe confcience. But this fecond time was alfo the laft: for Mifs Lambercier, perceiving, doubtlefs, by fome fign, that the chaftifement did not anfwer the intention, declared fhe renounced it, and that it wearied her too much. Until then we lay in her chamber, and in the winter fometimes even in her bed. Two days after we were removed to another room, and I had in future the honour, which I could very well have done without, of being treated by her as a great boy.

Who would believe it, that this childifh chaftifement, received at eight years old from the hand of a girl of thirty, fhould decide my taftes, my defires, my paffions, for the reft of my days, and that precifely in a contrary

sense

fenfe to what might have been expected naturally to follow it? At the very time my fenfes were fired, my defires took fo oppofite a turn, that, confined to what they had experienced, they fought no farther. With blood boiling with fenfuality almoft from my birth, I preferved my purity from every blemifh, even until the age when the coldeft and backwardeft conflitutions difcover themfelves. Long tormented, without knowing by what, I devoured with an ardent eye every fine woman, my imagination recalled them inceffantly to my memory, folely to fubmit them to my manner, and transform them into fo many Mifs Lamberciers.

Even after the marriageable age, this odd tafte, always encreafing, carried even to depravity, even to folly, preferved my morals good, the very reverfe of which might have been expected. If ever an education was modeft and chafte, 'twas certainly that I received. My three aunts were not only people of an exemplary prudence, but of a referve women have long fince forgot. My father, a man of pleafure, but gallant after the old fafhion, never advanced to thofe he loved a word which could make a virgin blufh, and never, than in our family and before me, was fhewn more of that refpect we owe children. The fame attention was found at Mr Lambercier's on that article; a very good maid-fervant was difcharged for a word a little waggifh fhe pronounced in our prefence. Not only I had no diftinct idea of the union of the fexes at the age of adolefcence, but the confufed idea
never

never prefented itfelf to me but as odious and difguftful. I had an averfion for public women, which never wore away, I could not fee a debauched fellow without difdain, nor even without terror, for my abhorrence of debauchery was carried to this point, fince, in going one day to the little Sacconex through a hollow way, I faw on each fide cavities in the earth, where I was told thefe people copulated. What I had feen amongft dogs always ftruck me in thinking of others, and my ftomach turned at this fole remembrance.

Thefe prejudices of education, proper in themfelves to retard the firft explofions of a combuftible conftitution, were aided, as I have already faid, by a diverfion caufed in me by the firft motions of fenfuality. Imagining no more than I felt, in fpite of the effervefcence of troublefome blood, I knew not how to carry my defires but towards that fpecies of voluptuoufnefs I was acquainted with, without quite reaching that which had been rendered hateful to me, and which drew fo near the other, without my ever fufpecting it. In my ftupid fancies, in my erotic fury, in the extravagant acts to which they fometimes carried me, I borrowed, in imagination, the affiftance of the other fex, without fuppofing it fit for any other ufe than that I burned to make of it.

I not only therefore thus paffed my whole age of puberty with a conftitution extremely ardent, extremely lafcivious, and extremely forward, without defiring, without the knowledge of any other fatisfaction of the fenfes than thofe Mifs Lambercier innocently gave
me

me an idea of; but when at laſt the progreſs
of years had made me a man, it was that
which might have deſtroyed me, that ſaved
me.   My old childiſh taſte, inſtead of vaniſh-
ing, ſo aſſociated with the other, I could never
remove it from thoſe deſires fired by the ſenſes;
and this folly, joined to my natural timidity,
has always rendered me very little enterpriſing
with women, for fear of ſaying all or not being able to do all, that ſort of enjoyment,
whereof the other was to me but the laſt ſtage,
not being to be uſurped by him who deſires,
or gueſſed at by her who can grant it.   I have
thus paſſed my days in coveting and in ſilence
with thoſe I moſt loved.   Never daring to
declare my taſte, I at leaſt amuſed it by relations which preſerved its idea.   To fall at the
feet of an imperious miſtreſs, obey her orders,
have pardons to aſk her, were for me the ſweet-
eſt enjoyments, and the more my lively imagination enflamed my blood, the more I had the
air of a whining lover.   It is conceived this
manner of making love is not attended by a
rapid progreſs, nor is very dangerous to the virtue of its object.   I have therefore poſſeſſed
little, but have not been without enjoyment,
in my manner; that is imaginary.   Thus
have the ſenſes, agreeing with my timid humour and romantic mind, preſerved my feelings pure and my morals chaſte, by the ſame
inclinations which, perhaps, with a little more
effrontery, might have plunged me into the
moſt brutal pleaſures

    I have made the firſt ſtep and the moſt pain-
ful in the obſcure and dirty maze of my Con-
feſſions.

feſſions. 'Tis not criminality we are moſt unwilling to divulge, 'tis what is moſt ridiculous and ſhameful. Henceforward I am ſure of myſelf, after what I have dared to diſcloſe, nothing can be able to ſtop me. You may judge how much ſuch acknowledgements coſt me, ſince, during the whole courſe of my life, hurried ſometimes away with thoſe I loved, by the fury of a paſſion which deprived me of the faculty of ſight, of hearing, out of my ſenſes, and ſeized with a convulſive trembling all over my body, I could never take upon me to declare my folly, and to implore, during the moſt intimate familiarity, the only favour to be added to the reſt. It never happened but once in my childhood, with a child of my age beſides, ſhe it was who firſt propoſed it

In thus remounting to the firſt traces of my ſenſible being, I find elements, which, ſeeming ſometimes incompatible, have not a little united to produce with force an uniform and ſimple effect, and I find others which, the ſame in appearance, have formed, by the concurrence of certain circumſtances, ſo different combinations, that one would never imagine they had the leaſt reſemblance to each other. Who would believe, for inſtance, that one of the moſt vigorous ſprings of my ſoul was tempered in the ſame ſource from which luxury and eaſe was communicated to it? Without abandoning the ſubject I have juſt ſpoken of, I will ſhew you a very different impreſſion it made.

I was one day ſtudying alone in a chamber contiguous to the kitchen; the maid had put
ſome

fome of Mifs Lambercier's combs to dry by
the fire, when fhe came to fetch them, fhe
found the teeth of one of them broke. who
fufpect of this havock? None befides myfelf
had entered the room: they queftion me; I
deny having touched the comb, Mr. and Mifs
Lambercier confult, exhort, prefs, threaten;
I perfift obftinately, but conviction was too
ftrong, and carried it againft all my proteftations, though this was the firft time they caught
me in fo audacious lies. The affair was
thought ferious; it deferved it. The wicked-
nefs, the lie, the obftinacy, were thought
equally worthy of punifhment; but this time
it was not Mifs Lambercier that inflicted it.
My uncle Bernard was wrote to; he came.
My poor coufin was charged with another
crime not lefs ferious; we were taken to the
fame execution. It was terrible. If, feeking
the remedy even in the evil, they had intended
for ever to allay my depraved fenfes, they could
not have taken a fhorter method; and I affure
you, they left me a long time at peace.

They could not force from me the acknow-
ledgement they fought: this renewed feveral
times, and thrown into the moft dreadful fituation, I was immoveable. I would have fuffered death, and was refolved on it. Force itfelf was obliged to yield to the diabolical infatuation of a child, for no other name was
given to my conftancy. In fine, I came out
of this cruel trial in pieces, but triumphant.

It is now near fifty years fince this adventure, and I am not afraid of being in future
punifhed for the fame fact. Well, I declare in
the

the face of heaven, I was innocent; that I neither broke nor touched the comb; that I never came near the fire, nor ever thought of it. Let me not be afked how it happened; I know not, nor can comprehend it, all that I know of it is that I was innocent.

Figure to yourfelf a timid and docile character in common life, but ardent, haughty, invincible in his paffions, a child always governed by the voice of reafon, always treated with mildnefs, equity, and complaifance; who had not even the idea of injuftice, and who, for the firft time, experiences fo terrible a one, from thofe, precifely, he moft cherifhes and refpects. What a perverting of ideas! what a diforder in the fentiments! what confufion in the heart, in the brain, in all one's little being, intelligent and moral! I fay, let any one imagine to themfelves all this, if poffible, for as to myfelf, I am not capable of difcovering or following the leaft trace of what paffed in me at the time.

I had not reafon enough to feel how much appearances condemned me, and to put myfelf in the place of others; I kept to my own, and all I felt was the rigour of a dreadful chaftifement for a crime I had not committed. The forenefs of my body, though violent, I fcarcely felt, I only felt indignation, rage, and defpair. My coufin, in almoft a like cafe, who had been punifhed for an involuntary fault as a premeditated act, grew furious by my example, and raifed himfelf in a manner to unite with me. Both in the fame bed embraced each other with convulfive tranfports, we were fuffocated;
and

and when our young hearts, a little eafed, could breathe out their indignation, we fat up in our bed, and began both of us crying out, an hundred times, with all our force, Carnifex ! Carnifex ! Carnifex !

I feel in writing this my pulfe ftill rife; thefe moments would be continually prefent, were I to live an hundred thoufand years. This firft fentiment of violence and of injuftice is fo deeply graven on my foul, that every refembling idea brings back my firft emotion ; and this fentiment relative to me in its origin, has taken fuch a confiftence, and is fo far from perfonal intereft, that my heart is inflamed at the fight or recital of an unjuft action, whatever may be its object, or wherefoever it may be committed, as if the effect fell on me. When I read the hiftory of a cruel tyrant, the fubtle black actions of a knavifh prieft, I could fet off heartily to ftab thefe mifcreants, though I fhould perifh an hundred times in the attempt. I have often fweated in purfuing and ftoning a cock, a cow, a dog, an animal, I faw torment another, only becaufe he knew himfelf to be the ftrongeft. This emotion may be natural to me, and I believe it is ; but the profound remembrance of the firft injuftice I fuffered, was too long and too ftrongly annexed not to have greatly ftrengthened it.

This was the end of my childifh ferenity. From this moment I ceafed to enjoy pure happinefs, and I feel even at this inftant the remembrance of the charms of childhood ftops there. We remained at Boffey a few months afterwards. We were there, as the firft man is reprefented in the terreftrial paradife, but having ceafed to enjoy it. It was in appearance the fame fituation, but in effect quite another fort of being. Attachment, refpect, intimacy, confidence, no longer bound the pupils to their guides; we no longer thought them gods who could read our hearts; we were lefs afhamed to do wrong, and more fearful of being accufed; we began to be fly, to mutter, and to lie. All the vices of our age corrupted our innocence and clouded our diverfions; even the country loft in our eyes its alluring fweetnefs and fimplicity which reach the heart: it feemed to us defert and gloomy; it was, as it were, covered with a veil which hid its beauties. We ceafed to cultivate our little gardens, our herbs, and our flowers. We no more went to fcrape up the earth, and cry out with joy, on difcovering a fhoot of the grain we had fown. We grew diffatisfied with this life; they grew tired of us, my uncle took us home, and we feparated from Mifs Lambercier, cloyed with each other, and little regretting our feparation.

Near thirty years have paffed away fince I left Boffey, without having recollected my abode there, in an agreeable manner, by a remembrance a little coherent: but fince I have paffed the prime of life, and am declining towards old-age, I feel the fame remembrance of things fpring up again, while others wear away, and imprint themfelves in my memory with a charm and a force which daily increafes; as if finding already life flying from me, I feek to catch hold of it again, by its commencement.

ment. The leaſt facts of thoſe times pleaſed me
for no other reaſon than that they were of thoſe
times. I recollect *every circumſtance of places,
perſons*, and hours. I ſee the maid or the
footman buſy in the chamber, a ſwallow coming in at the window, a fly ſettling on my
hand, while I was ſaying my leſſon : I ſee the
whole arrangement of the room we were in ;
M. Lambercier's cloſet on the right, a print
repreſenting all the popes, a barometer, a large
calendar ; raſpberry-trees which, from a very
elevated garden, in which the houſe ſtood low
in the back of it, ſhaded the window, and
ſometimes came quite in. I know the reader
has no occaſion to be acquainted with all this ;
but I have occaſion myſelf to tell it him Why
am I aſhamed to relate equally every little
anecdote of my happy years, which yet make
me leap with joy when I recollect them. Five
or ſix particularly——Let us compound. I
will leave out five, but I will have one, only
one ; provided you let me lengthen it as much
as poſſible, to prolong my pleaſure.

If I ſought yours only, I might chuſe that
of Miſs Lambercier's backſide, which, by an
unlucky fall at the bottom of the meadow,
was expoſed quite bare to the king of Sardinia, as he was paſſing : but that of the walnut-
tree on the terrace is more amuſing to me,
who was the actor, whereas at the fall I was
only a ſpectator ; and I own I could not find
the leaſt cauſe for laughing at an accident
which, though odd in itſelf, alarmed me for a
perſon I loved as my mother, and perhaps
more.

VOL. I.   C   O you

O you curious readers of the grand hiſtory of the walnut-tree on the terrace, liſten to the horrible tragedy, and abſtain from trembling if you can

There was on the outſide of the court-door a terrace on the left hand on coming in, on which they often ſat after dinner, but it had no ſhade. that it might have ſome, M. Lambercier had a walnut-tree planted there. The planting it was attended with ſolemnity the two boarders were the godfathers, and whilſt they were filling the hole, we each of us held the tree with one hand, ſinging ſongs of triumph. It was watered by a ſort of baſon round its foot. Every day, ardent ſpectators of this watering, we confirmed each other, my couſin and me, in a very natural idea, that it was nobler to plant trees on the terrace than colours on a breach, and we reſolved to procure ourſelves this glory, without dividing it with any one.

To do this, we went and cut the ſlips of a willow, and planted it on the terrace, at eight or ten feet from the auguſt walnut-tree. We did not forget to make likewiſe a hollow round our tree, the difficulty lay in getting wherewithal to fill it, for water was brought from a conſiderable diſtance, and we were not permitted to go out to fetch it. however, it was' abſolutely wanting to our willow. We made uſe of every wile to let it have ſome for a few days, and we ſo well ſucceeded, we ſaw it bud and throw out ſmall leaves, whoſe growth was meaſured from hour to hour, perſuaded, though

it

it was not a foot from the ground, it would not be long before it shaded us.

As our tree, taking up our whole time, rendered us incapable of any other application, of all study, we were as in a delirium, and the cause not being known, we were kept closer than before ; we saw the fatal moment wherein our water would fall short, and were afflicted with the expectation of seeing our tree perish with drought. At last, necessity, the mother of industry, suggested an invention of saving our tree and ourselves from certain death, it was to make under ground a furrow which would privately conduct to the willow a part of the water they brought the walnut-tree. This undertaking, executed with ardour, did not succeed immediately. we took our descent so badly, the water did not run, the earth fell in and stopt up the furrow ; the entrance was filled with filth, all went cross. Nothing dispirited us. *Omnia vincit labor improbus.* We cut our earth and our bason deeper to let the water run, we cut the bottom of boxes into little narrow planks, whereof some laid flat in a row, and others forming an angle from each side of them, made us a triangular channel for our conduit. At the entrance we placed small ends of thin wood, not close, which, forming a kind of grate, kept back the mud and stones without stopping the water We carefully covered our work over with well-trodden earth, and the day it was finished, we waited, in agonies of hope and fear, the hour of watering. After ages of expectation, this hour at last came: M. Lambercier came also as usual to affift at the performance, during which we got both of us behind him to hide our tree, to which happily he turned his back.

They had fcarcely begun pouring the firft pail of water, but we began to perceive it run to our bafon· at this fight prudence abanboned us, we fet up fhouts of joy, which caufed M. Lambercier to turn round—it was a pity; for he was pleafing himfelf greatly to fee how greedily the earth of his walnut-tree fwallowed the water. Struck at feeing it divide itfelf between two bafons, he fhouts in his turn, fees; perceives the roguery; orders, in hafte, a pick-axe, gives a ftroke, makes two or three of our planks fly, and hallooing with all his ftrength, *An aquiduct! an aqueduct!* he ftrikes on every fide unmerciful ftrokes, every one of which reached the bottom of our hearts. In one moment the planking, the conduit, the bafon, the willow, all were deftroyed, all plowed up, without there having been pronounced, during this terrible expedition, any other word than the exclamation he inceffantly repeated· *An aqueduct!* cried he, at the fame time breaking up all, *an aqueduct! an aqueduct!*

You would think the adventure ended badly for the young architects. You miftake: the whole ended there. M. Lambercier never reproached us of it, did not fhew us a different countenance, and faid no more of it to us, we even heard him foon after laugh with his fifter with all his might; for the laugh of M. Lambercier was heard afar, and, what is more aftonifhing, after the firft fenfation, we ourfelves were

were not afflicted. We planted in another place another tree, and often called to mind the catastrophe of the first, repeating with emphasis to ourselves, *An aqueduct ! an aqueduct !* Till then I had fits of pride, by intervals, when I was Aristides or Brutus. This was my first movement of vanity quite visible. To have constructed an aqueduct with my own hands, having put a slip of wood in concurrence with a large tree, appeared to me a supreme degree of glory. At ten I judged better than Cæsar at thirty.

The idea of this walnut tree, and the little history it relates to, was so well retained in my memory, that one of my most agreeable projects in my journey to Geneva in 1754, was to go to Bossey, and review my childish amusements, and particularly the beloved walnut-tree, which must at that time have been the third of a century old. I was so continually beset, and so little my own master, I could not obtain a moment to satisfy myself. There is little appearance of the occasion ever being renewed. I have not, however, lost the desire with the hope, and I am almost certain, if ever I return to these charming spots, and should find my beloved walnut-tree still existing, I should water it with my tears.

Returned to Geneva, I passed two or three years at my uncle's, waiting till they should resolve what to do with me. As he devoted his son to genius, he was instructed in a little drawing, and he taught him himself the Elements of Euclid. I learnt all this being a companion, and it took my taste, particularly drawing. However,

it

it was debated, whether I was to be watch-maker, lawyer, or a minister. I liked best to be a minister, for I thought it very clever to preach, but the little income left by my mother, which was to be divided between my brother and me, was not sufficient to support my studies. As my age did not render the choice very pressing, I remained in the mean while with my uncle, losing, nearly. my time, not without paying, very justly, pretty dear for my board.

My uncle, a man of pleasure as well as my father, knew not like him how to submit to his duties, and took very little care of us My aunt was devout, even a pietist, who preferred singing psalms to our education they left us almost at an entire liberty, which we never abused Always inseparable, we sufficed to each other, and not being inclined to frequent the rakes of our age, we learned none of those habits of libertinism our idle life might have prompted us to. I am to blame even to suppose us idle, for in our lives we were never less so, and the greatest happiness was, that every amusement which we successively pursued, kept us together employed in the house, without being inclined ever to go into the street. We made cages, pipes, kites, drums, houses, ships, and bows. We spoiled the tools of my good old grandfather, to make watches in imitation of him We had particularly a taste of preference to daubing paper, drawing, washing, colouring, and spoiling colours. There came an Italian mountebank to Geneva, called Gamba Corta, we went once to see him, but would go no more. he had puppets—so we
set

set ourselves to making puppets; his puppets played a kind of comedy, and we made comedies for ours For want of the practical, we counterfeited in our throat Punch's voice, to act these charming comedies , our good parents had the patience to see and hear . but my uncle Bernard having one day read to his family a fine sermon of his, we left our comedies, and began to compose sermons. These details are not very interesting, I allow , but it shews how much our first education must have been well directed, as that, masters almost of our time, and of ourselves in an age so tender, we were so little tempted to abuse it. We had so little need of play fellows, we even neglected the occasion of seeking for them When we were taking our walk, we regarded their play as we passed without coveting it, without even thinking of taking part in it. Friendship so much filled our hearts, it sufficed to be together that the simplest tastes should be our delight.

By being continually together we were remarked , the more so, as, my cousin being very tall and I very little, it made a couple pleasantly sorted His long slender carcase, his small visage like a baked apple, his heavy air, his supine walk, excited the children to ridicule him. In the gibberish of the country, they gave him the nick-name of Barnâ Bredanna , and the moment we were out we heard nothing but Barnâ Bredanna all around us He suffered it easier than I : I was vexed ; I wanted to fight ; it was what the young rogues wanted. I fought, I was beat. My poor cousin gave me all the assistance in his

C 4 power;

power; but he was weak, at one ſtroke they knocked him down. 'Twas then I became furious. However, though I received ſome ſmart blows, 'twas not at me they were aimed, 'twas at Barnà Bredanna ; but I ſo far encreaſed the evil by my mutinous paſſion, we could ſtir out no more but when they were at ſchool, for fear of being hooted and followed by the ſcholars.

I am already become a redreſſer of grievances. To be a knight-erriant in form, I only wanted a lady. I had two. I went from time to time to ſee my father at Nion, a ſmall city in the Vaudois country, where he was ſettled. My father was much eſteemed, and kindneſs was extended to his ſon on that account. During the ſhort ſtay I made with him, 'twas who could receive me beſt. A Madam de Vulſon particularly ſhewed me a thouſand kindneſſes, and, to fill up the meaſure, her daughter made me her gallant. Any one can tell what a gallant at eleven is to a girl of two-and-twenty. But theſe rogues are ſo glad to put their little puppets in the front to hide the great ones, or to tempt them by the ſhow of a paſtime they ſo well know how to render alluring. For my part, who ſaw between her and me no inequality, I took it up ſeriouſly, I gave into it with my whole heart, or rather with my whole head ; for I was very little amorous elſewhere, though I was ſo even to madneſs, and that my tranſports, my agitations, and my fury, raiſed ſcenes that would make you die of laughing.

I am acquainted with two ſorts of love, very diſtinct, very real, but not in the leaſt allied,
                                                            though

though each are extremely violent, and both differ from tender friendſhip. The whole courſe of my life has been divided between theſe two loves of ſo different a nature, and I have even experienced them both at the ſame time; for inſtance, at the time I ſpeak of, whilſt I ſo publicly claimed Miſs de Vulſon ſo tyrannically that I could ſuffer no man to approach her, I had with Miſs Goton meetings that were ſhort enough, but pretty paſſionate, in which ſhe thought proper to act the ſchoolmiſtreſs, and that was every thing; but this every thing, which was in fact every thing to me, appeared to me ſupreme happineſs; and already perceiving the value of the myſtery, though I knew how to uſe it only as a child, I reſtored back to Miſs Vulſon, who did not much expect it, the trouble ſhe took in employing me to hide other amours.   But, to my great mortification, my ſecret was diſcovered, or not ſo well kept by my little ſchoolmiſtreſs as by me, for we were ſoon ſeparated.

This Miſs Goton was in truth a ſingular perſon   Though not handſome, ſhe had ſomething difficult to be forgot, and that I too often, for an old fool, call yet to mind.   Her eyes, in particular, were not of her age, or ſtature, or carriage.   She had a little impoſing and lofty air, extremely well adapted to her part, and which occaſioned the firſt idea of any thing between us.   But that moſt extraordinary in her was a mixture of impudence and reſerve, difficult to conceive.   She permitted herſelf the greateſt familiarities with me, but never permitted me any with her; ſhe treated me exactly as a child This makes me think, she had either ceafed to be one, or that, on the contrary, she herfelf was ftill fufficiently fo, as to perceive no more than play in the dangei to which she expofed herfelf.

I belonged in a manner to each of thefe people, and fo entirely, that with either of them I never thought of the other But as to the reft, no refemblance in what they made me feel for them. I could have paffed my days with Mifs Vulfon without a thought of leaving her; but on feeing her, my joy was calm, and did not reach emotion. I was particularly fond of her in a great company; her pleafantries, her ogling, even jealoufy attached me to her: I triumphed with pride at a preference to great rivals she feemed to me to ufe ill. I was tortured, but I liked the torture Applaufe, encouragement, fmiles, heated me, animated me. I was paffionate and furious; I was tranfported with love in a cucle. Tête-a-tête I should have been conftrained, dull, and perhaps forrowful. However, I felt tenderly for her; I fuffered if she was ill. I would have given my health to eftablish hers; and obferve that I knew by experience what good and bad health was. Abfent, I thought of her, she was wanting; prefent, her careffes came foft to my heart, not to my fenfe. I was familiar to her with impunity; my imagination afked nothing but she granted I could, however, not have fupported her doing as much for others. I loved her as a brother, but was jealous as a lover.

I should

I should have been so of Miss Goton as a Turk, a fury, or a tiger, had I only imagined she could grant others the same favours she did me; for these were asked even on my knees. I approached Miss de Vulson with an active pleasure, but without uneasness; but at the sight of Miss Goton I was bewildered; every sense was overturned. I was familiar with the former, without taking liberties; on the contrary, trembling and agitated before the latter, even in the height of familiarity. I believe, had I remained too long with her, I could not have been able to live, my palpitations would have smothered me. I equally dreaded displeasing them, but was more complaisant to one, and more submissive to the other. I would not have angered Miss Vulson for the world, but if Miss Goton had commanded me to throw myself in the flames, I think I should instantly have obeyed her.

. My amours, or rather my rendezvous with her, did not continue long, happily for her and me. Though my connections with Miss Vulson were not so dangerous, they were not without their catastrophe, after having lasted a little longer. The end of these affairs ought always to have an air a little romantic, and cause exclamation. Though my correspondence with Miss Vulson was less active, it was perhaps more endearing. We never separated without tears, and it is singular in what a burdensome void I found myself, whenever I left her. I could talk of nothing but her, or think of any thing but her, my sorrows were real and lively, but I believe, at bottom, these

heroic

heroic forrows were not all for her, and that, without perceiving it, amufement, of which fhe was the centre, bore a good fhare in them. To foften the rigour of abfence, we wrote each other letters, pathetical enough to fplit rocks. In fine, I had the glory of her not being able longer to hold out, and fhe came to fee me at Geneva. This once my head was quite gone ; I was intoxicated and mad the two days fhe ftaid. When fhe departed, I would have thrown myfelf into the water after her, and long did the air refound with my cries. The following week fhe fent me fweetmeats and gloves, which would have appeared gallant, had I not at the fame time learnt her marriage, and that this journey, of which I thought proper to give myfelf the honour, was to buy her wedding-fuit. I fhall not defcribe my fury ; it is conceived. I fwore in my noble rage never more to fee the perfidious girl ; thinking fhe could not fuffer a greater punifh-ment. However, it did not occafion her death ; for twenty years afterwards, on a vifit to my father, being with him on the lake, I afked who were thofe ladies we faw in a boat not far from ours. How, fays my father, fmiling, does not your heart tell you ? Thefe are thy ancient amours, 'tis Madam Chriftin, 'tis Mifs de Vulfon. I ftarted at the almoft for-gotten name, but I told the waterman to turn off, not judging it worth while, though I had a fine opportunity of revenging myfelf, to be perjured, and to renew a difpute twenty years paft with a woman of forty.

Thus

Thus did I lose in foolery the most precious time of my childhood, before my destination was determined. After great deliberation on my natural dispositions, they determined on what was the most repugnant to them : I was sent to a M. Masseron, register of the city, to learn under him, as M. Bernard said, the useful science of a scraper. This nick-name displeased me sovereignly ; the hopes of heaping money by ignoble means flattered but little my lofty temper; the employment appeared to me tiresome and insupportable; the assiduity and subjection completed my disgust, and I never went into the place where the registers are kept, but with a horror that encreased from day to day. M. Masseron, on his part, little satisfied with me, treated me with disdain, incessantly upbraiding me as a fool and a blockhead ; repeating daily that my uncle assured I was *knowing, knowing*, whilst in fact I knew nothing ; that he had promised him a sprightly boy, and had sent him an ass. In fine, I was turned out of the Rolls ignominiously as a fool, and the clerks of M. Masseron pronounced me fit for nothing but to handle the file.

My vocation thus determined, I was bound apprentice ; not however to a watchmaker, but to an engraver. The contempt of the register humbled me extremely, and I obeyed without murmur. My master, named M. Ducommun, was a boorish, violent young man, who made a shift, in a very little time, to tarnish all the splendour of my childhood, to stupify my amiable and sprightly disposition, and to reduce my senses as well as my fortune to the true state

of

of an apprentice. My Latin, my antiquities, h'ſtory, all was for a long time forgotten : I did not even remember the world had ever produced Romans. My father, when I went to ſee him, ſaw no longer his idol ; the ladies found nothing of the gallant Jean-Jacques ; and I was myſelf ſo well convinced that Mr. and Miſs Lambercier would no longer receive me as their pupil, that I was aſhamed to be ſeen by them ; and ſince that time have I never ſeen them. The vileſt inclinations, the baſeſt tricks, ſucceeded my amiable amuſements, without leaving me the leaſt idea of them. I muſt have had, in ſpite of my good education, a great inclination to degenerate ; for I did ſo in the moſt rapid manner, and without the leaſt trouble, and never did ſo forward a Cæſar ſo quickly become a Landon.

The art itſelf did not diſpleaſe me ; I had a lively taſte for drawing, the exerciſe of the graver pleaſed me well enough, and as the talent of a watch-caſe engraver is very confined, I hoped to attain perfection. I ſhould have reach'd it, perhaps, if the brutality of my maſter, and exceſſive conſtraint, had not diſguſted me with labour. I waſted his time, to employ it in occupations of my own ſort, but which had in my eyes the charms of liberty I engraved a kind of medals to ſerve me and my companions as an order of chivalry. My maſter ſurprized me at this contraband labour, and broke my bones, telling me I exerciſed myſelf in coining money, becauſe our medals bore the arms of the republic. I can ſafely ſwear I had not the leaſt idea of counterfeit, and very little of the real money.

I knew

I knew better how to make a Roman As, than one of our three-penny pieces.

My master's tyranny rendered the labour I should otherwise have loved infupportable, and drove me to vices I should have defpifed, fuch as falfehood, lazinefs, and theft. Nothing has fo well taught me the difference between filial dependence and fervile flavery, as the remembrance of the change it produced in me at this period. Naturally timid and bafhful, no one fault was fo diftant from me as effrontery. But I enjoyed a decent liberty, which had only been reftrained 'till then by degrees, and at laft entirely vanifhed. I was bold at my father's, free at M. Lambercier's, difcreet at my uncle's; I became fearful at my mafters, and from that time was a loft child. Accuftomed to a perfect equality with my fuperiors in their method of living, never to know a pleafure I could not command, to fee no difh of which I did not partake, to have no wifh but was made known, to bring, in fine, every motion of my heart to my lips, judge what I muft be reduced to in a houfe where I dare not open my mouth, where I muft leave the table without half filling my belly, and quit the room when I had nothing to do there, either inceffantly chained to my work, feeing nothing but objects of enjoyment for others, and none for me; where the profpect of the liberty of my mafter and his journeymen encreafed the weight of my fubjection, where, in difputes on what I was beft acquainted with, I dare not fpeak; where, in fine, every thing I faw became for my heart an object I coveted for no other reafon
than

than becaufe I was deprived of it. Farewel
eafe, gaiety, happy expreffions, which before
often caufed my faults to efcape chaftifement.
I cannot recollect without laughing, that one
evening, at my father's, being ordered to bed
for fome prank without my fupper, and paffing
through the kitchen with my forry bit of bread,
I faw and fmelt the roaft meat turning on the
fpit People were round the fire; I muft bow to
every one as I paffed.   When I had been all
round, eying the roaft meat, which looked fo
nice, and fmelt fo well, I could not abftain from
making that likewife a bow, and telling it, in a
pitiful tone, Good bye roaft meat! This fally
of ingenuity appeared fo pleafant, it procured
my ftay to fupper. Perhaps it might have had
the effect at my mafter's; but it is certain it
would not have come to my mind, or that
I had not dared to deliver it

'Twas by this method I learnt to covet in
filence, to be fly, diffimulate, lie, and to fteal
at laft, a thought which till then never ftruck
me, and of which fince that time I could not
entirely cure myfelf. Covetoufnefs and inabi-
lity to attain always leads there. This is the
reafon all footmen are thieves, and why all
apprentices are fo; but in an even and tranquil
fituation, when every thing they fee is at command, they rofe, as they grow up, this fhame-
ful propenfity. Not having had the fame advantage, I could not have the fame benefit.

It is almoft always good fentiments badly
directed which turns children's firft fteps to ill.
In fpite of the continual wants and temptations, I had been near a year without being
                                        able

able to refolve on taking any thing, not even eatables. My firft theft was an affair of complaifance; but it opened the door to others, which had not fo commendable an end.

There was a journeyman at my mafter's, named M. Verrat, whofe houfe, in the neighbourhood, had a garden at a confiderable diftance, which produced exceeding fine afparagus. M. Verrat, who had not much money, took in his head to rob his mother of her forward afparagus, and fell them for a few hearty breakfafts. As he did not chufe to expofe himfelf, and was not very nimble, he chofe me for this expedition. After a little preliminary flattery, which won me fo much the readier as I did not perceive its end, he propofed it as an idea which that moment ftruck him. I oppofed it greatly; he infifted. I never could refift flattery; I fubmitted I went every morning and gathered the fineft afparagus; I carried them to the Molard, where fome good old woman, perceiving I had juft ftolen them, told me fo to get them cheaper. In my fright I took what they would give me; I carried it to M. Verrat. It was foon metamorphofed into a breakfaft, whereof I was the purveyor, and which he divided with another companion; for, as to me, very happy in a trifling bribe, I did not touch even their wine.

This game went on feveral days before it came into my mind to rob the robber, and to tythe M. Verrat's harveft of afparagus. I executed my roguery with the greateft fidelity; my only motive was to pleafe him who fet me

to

to work. If, however, I had been taken, what a drubbing, what abuse, what cruel treatment fhould not I have undergone, while the mifcreant, in belying me, would have been believed on his word, and I doubly punifhed for having dared to accufe him, becaufe he was a journeyman, and I an apprentice only. Thus, in every ftate, the great rogue faves himfelf at the expence of the feeble innocent one.

I thus learnt that it was not fo terrible to thieve as I imagined, and I made fo good a ufe of my fcience, that nothing I wifhed for within my reach was in fafety. I was not abfolutely badly fed at my mafter's, and fobriety was no otherwife painful to me, than becaufe I faw him keep fo little within its bounds. The cuftom of fending young people from table when thofe things are ferved up which tempt them moft, appeared to me well adapted to render them as liquorifh as knavifh I became, in a fhort time, the one and the other, and found it anfwer pretty well in general; fometimes very ill, when I was found out.

A recollection which makes me even now fhudder and fmile at the fame time, is of an apple hunt which coft me dear. Thefe apples were at the bottom of a pantry, which by an high lattice received light from the kitchen. One day, being alone in the houfe, I climbed the maypole to fee in the garden of the Hefperides the precious fruit I could not approach. I fetched the fpit to fee if it would reach fo far: it was too fhort. I lengthened it with
                                              another

another little spit which was used for small
game; for my master loved hunting. I
pricked at them several times without success;
at last I felt with transport I was bringing an
apple. I drew it very gently; the apple
already touched the lattice; I was going to
seize it. Who can express my grief? The
apple was too big; it would not pass through
the hole. What invention did I not make
use of to pull it through? I was obliged to
seek supporters to keep the spit right, a knife
long enough to split the apple, a lath to hold
it up. At length by schemes and time I at-
tained its division, hoping afterwards to draw
the pieces one after the other. But they were
scarcely divided when they both fell into the
pantry. Compassionate reader, partake of my
affliction!

I did not lose courage; but I lost a deal of
time. I dreaded being surprized; I put off
'till the morrow a happier trial; I return to
my work as if nothing had happened, without
thinking of the two indiscreet witnesses of
my transaction, which I had left in the
pantry.

The next day, seeing a fine opportunity, I
make the other trial. I get up on my stool,
I lengthen the spit, I aim, am just going to
prick . . . . . unfortunately the dragon did not
sleep; all at once the pantry door opens; my
master comes out, crosses his arms, looks at
me, and says Bravo! . . . . The pen drops out
of my hand.

Very soon, by continual bad treatment, I
grew less feeling . it seemed to me a sort of
com-

compenſation for theft, which gave me a right
to continue it. Inſtead of looking back at
the puniſhment, I looked forward on the revenge. I judged that to beat me like a
ſcoundrel, gave me a right to be ſo. I ſaw
that to rob and to be beat went together, and
conſtituted a ſort of trade, and that by fulfilling
that part of it which depended on me, I might
leave the care of the other to my maſter. On
this idea, I ſet to thieving with more tranquillity than before. I ſaid to myſelf, What will
be the conſequence? I know the worſt; I
ſhall be beat. ſo be it; I am made for it

I love to eat without avidity; I am ſenſual,
but not greedy. Too many other taſtes take
that away from me. I never employed my
thoughts on my appetite but when my heart
was unoccupied; and this has ſo rarely happened, I ſeldom had time to think of good-
eating. This was the reaſon I did not long
confine myſelf to thieving eatables; I ſoon
extended it to every thing I liked; and if I
did not become a robber in form, 'twas becauſe
money never much tempted me. In the common room my maſter had a private cloſet
locked, I found means to open the door, and
ſhut it again, without its appearing. There I
laid under contribution his beſt tools, his
fine drawings, his impreſſions, all I had any
mind to, and that he affected to keep from
me. Theſe thefts were innocent at the bottom, as they were employed in his ſervice;
but I was tranſported with joy at having theſe
trifles in my power; I thought I ſtole the
talent with its productions. Beſides, he had

in

in his boxes the filings of gold and silver, small jewels, pieces of value, and money. If I had four or five sous in my pocket, 'twas a great deal : however, far from touching, I don't recollect having glanced a wishful look at any of those things. I saw them with more terror than pleasure. I verily believe this dread of taking money and what produces it, was caused in a great measure by education. There were mixt with it secret ideas of infamy, prison, punishment, gallows, which would have made me tremble, had I been tempted , whereas my tricks appeared to me no more than waggery, and in fact were nothing else. The whole could occasion but a good trimming from my master, and I was prepared for that before-hand.

But once more, I say, I did not covet sufficiently to make me abstain ; I saw nothing to dread. A sheet only of fine drawing-paper tempted me more than the money which would purchase a ream. This humour is the effect of one of the singularities of my character ; and has had so much influence on my conduct as to merit an explanation.

I have passions extremely violent, and, whilst they agitate me, nothing can equal my impetuosity : I am a total stranger to discretion, respect, fear, or decorum , I am rude, saucy, violent, and intrepid , no shame can stop me, no danger can affright me. Beyond the sole object that employs my mind, the whole world is nothing to me : but all this lasts but for a moment, and the moment following I am a worm. Take me in my calm moments,

moments, I am indolence and timidity itself: the leaſt thing ſtartles and diſheartens me; the humming of a fly makes me afraid; a word ſpoke, a ſhrug of the ſhoulders, alarms my lazineſs; fear and ſhame ſubdue me to ſuch a degree, that I ſhould be glad to hide myſelf from mortal eyes. When I am forced to act, I know not what to do; when forced to ſpeak, I have nothing to ſay; if I am looked at, I am put out of countenance. When I am in a paſſion, I find ſometimes enough to ſay; but in ordinary converſation I can find nothing, nothing at all . this is the ſole reaſon I find it inſupportable, becauſe I am obliged to talk.

Add to this, none of my moſt favourite taſtes conſiſt in things to be purchaſed. I want none but pure pleaſures, and money poiſons them all. I love, for inſtance, thoſe of the table, but not being able to ſuffer the conſtraint of good company, or the intemperance of taverns, I enjoy them only with a friend; for alone it is impoſſible my imagination being buſied on other things, I have no pleaſure in eating. If my heated blood demands women, my beating heart demands love Women who are to be bought have no charms for me; I doubt even whether my money would not be paid in vain. It is thus with every pleaſure within my reach : when they are not gratis, I find them inſipid. I am fond of things which are for none but thoſe who know how to enjoy them

Money never ſeemed to me ſo precious a thing as people think it : and more, it never
appeared

appeared to me a very convenient thing; it
is good for nothing of itself; to enjoy it, you
muſt transform it; you muſt buy, bargain, often be duped, pay dear, and be badly ſerved. I
want a thing good in quality, with my money
I am ſure to have it bad I buy a new-laid egg
dear, it is ſtale ; the beſt fruit, it is green, a
girl, ſhe is tainted.   I love good wine, but
where ſhall I get it?   At a wine-merchant's?
Do what I will, he will poiſon me.   Would I
be perfectly well ſerved?   What attention,
what trouble ! Make friends, correſpondents,
ſend meſſages, write, go, come, wait, and often
at laſt be deceived.   What trouble with my
money ! I fear it more than I love good wine.

    A thouſand times during my apprenticeſhip,
and ſince, I went out to buy ſomething nice. I
go near the paſtry-cook's, I perceive women
at the counter; I think I already ſee them
laugh, and make a jeſt among themſelves of
the little greedy-gut.   I paſs by a fruit-ſhop;
I leer ſideways at the fine pears, their ſavour is
tempting; two or three young people cloſe by
watch me; a man who knows me is at the
door, I ſee at a diſtance a girl coming; is it
not our maid? My near ſight preſents a thouſand illuſions.   I take all who paſs' for perſons
of my acquaintance. every where I am intimidated, reſtrained by ſome obſtacle. my wiſhes
increaſe with my ſhame, and I return at laſt
like a fool, devoured with luſt, having in my
pocket wherewithal to ſatisfy it, without daring to buy any thing.

    I ſhould enter into the moſt inſipid particu-
lars, was I to follow the uſe of my money, whether

whether by myfelf, whether by others; the trou
ble, the fhame, the repugnance, the inconvenience, the difgufts of all forts I have always
experienced. As I go on with my life, the
reader, getting acquainted with my humour,
will perceive all this without my fatiguing him
with the recital.

This underftood, one of my pretended con-
tradictions will be eafily comprehended, of re-
conciling an almoft fordid avarice with the
greateft contempt of money. 'Tis a moveable
of fo little ufe to me, I never think of defiring that I have not; and that, when I have
any, I keep it a long time without fpending it,
for want of knowing how to employ it to my
fancy   but does the agreeable and convenient
occafion offer? I make fo good ufe of it as to
empty my purfe without perceiving it. However, don't imagine that I have the trick of
fpending through oftentation, quite the reverfe; I lay it out privately and for my pleafure: inftead of glorying in expence, I hide
it. I fo well perceive that money is not for
my ufe, I am almoft afhamed to have any,
much more to make ufe of it. If I had ever
poffeffed an income fufficient to live commo-
dioufly, I fhould never, I am certain, have
been tempted to be avaricious. I fhould fpend
my whole income without feeking to encreafe
it   but my precarious fituation keeps me in
fear.   I adore liberty, I abhor conftraint,
trouble, or fubjection. As long as the money
lafts which I have in my purfe, it infures my
independence, it frees me from contriving to
get more, a neceffity I always detefted : but
for

for fear of feeing it end, I make much of it · the money we poffefs is the inftrument of liberty; that we purfue is the inftrument of flavery. This is the reafon I hold faft and covet nothing.

My difinterestedness is therefore nothing but lazinefs; the pleafure of having is not worth the trouble of acquiring, and my diffipation is likewife nothing but lazirefs: when the occafion of an agreeable expence offers, we cannot too readily lay hold of it. I am lefs tempted with money than things, for between money and the defired poffeffion there is always an intermediate ftate, but between the thing and its enjoyment there is none. I fee the thing, it tempts me, if I fee the means of acquiring it only, it does not tempt me.

I have therefore been a rogue, and am yet fometimes, for trifles which tempt me, and that I had rather take than afk for. But little or big, I never recollect having in my life taken a farthing from any one, except once, not fifteen years ago, I ftole feven livres ten fous. The ftory is worth telling; for there is feen in it a concurrence of impudence and ftupidity I fhould find fome difficulty to give credit to, had it regarded any one but myfelf.

It was at Paris. I was walking with M. de Francueil, at the Palais Royal, about five o'clock. He pulls out his watch, looks at it, and fays to me, Let us go to the opera. With all my heart. We go. He takes two box tickets, gives me one, and goes in firft with the other; I follow. In going in after him, I find the door crowded. I look; I fee every body up;

I judge I might be loft in the crowd, or at leaft give reafon to M. de Francueil to fuppofe me loft. I go out, afk for my ticket again, afterwards my money, and away I go, without thinking that I had fcarcely reached the door when every one was feated, and that M. de Francueil faw plainly I was not there.

As nothing was ever fo diftant from my humour as this behaviour, I note it, to fhew there are moments of a fort of delirium, when men are not to be judged by their actions. It was not precifely ftealing the money, 'twas ftealing the ufe of it · the lefs it was a robbery, the more infamous it was.

I fhould never end thefe accounts, was I to follow every track, through which, during my apprenticefhip, I paffed from the fublimity of a hero to the bafenefs of a villain However, in taking the vices of my condition, it was not poffible entirely to take its taftes. I grew tired of the amufements of my companions, and when too great reftraint had likewife difgufted me of work, every thing hung heavy. This renewed my inclination for ftudy, which had been long loft. Thofe ftudies, taking me off my work, became another crime, which brought on other punifhments. This inclination by conftraint became a paffion, and very foon a furious one. La Tribu, famous for letting out books, fupplied me with every kind of them. Good or bad, all went down; I never picked them. I read them all with the fame earneftnefs I read at my work, I read in going to do a meffage, I read in the neceffary, and forgot myfelf for hours fuccef-
fively;

sively; my brain was turned with reading; I did nothing but read. My master watched me, surprised me, beat me, took my books. How many volumes were there not torn, burned, and thrown out at window! What sets remained imperfect at La Tribu's! When I had no money, I gave her my shirts, my cravats, my clothes, and my allowance of three pence a week was regularly carried there.

Thus, therefore, I might be told, money is become necessary. True; but it was when reading had deprived me of all activity. Entirely given up to this new taste, I did nothing but read, I robbed no longer. This is another of my characteristic differences. In the heat of a certain habit of being, a nothing calls me off, changes me, fixes me, at last becomes passion, and then all is forgot. I think of nothing but the new object which employs me. My heart beat with desire to dip into the new book in my pocket, I pulled it out the instant I was alone, and thought no more of pilfering my master's closet. I don't think I should have robbed even if my passions had been more expensive. Confined to the present moment, it did not reach my turn of mind to provide for futurity. La Tribu gave me credit, it was but a trifle, and when once I had pocketed my book, I looked no further. Money that came to me naturally passed to this woman; and when she became pressing, nothing was at hand but my own things. To rob before-hand was too much foresight, and to rob to pay was no temptation.

By

By repeated quarrels, beatings, private and ill-chosen studies, my humour became reserved and wild, my head began to be impaired, and I led the life of an owl. However, though my taste did not preserve me from flat, unmeaning books, my good fortune preserved me from obscene and licentious ones, not but La Tribu, a woman in every respect very complaisant, would have made the least scruple at supplying me with them. But to raise their price, she named them with an air of mystery, which precisely forced me to refuse them, as much from disgust as shame, and chance so well seconded my modest humour, I was more than thirty years old before I first saw any one of these dangerous books.

In less than a year I ran through the thin shop of La Tribu, and then found my leisure hours cruelly unoccupied. Cured of my childish, rakish fancies by my taste for reading, and likewise by reading, which, though without choice, and often bad, brought back my heart, however, to nobler sentiments than my condition inspired, disgusted of all within my reach, and finding all that could tempt me, out of it; I saw nothing possible to flatter my heart. My senses, having beat high for some time, demanded an enjoyment of which I could not even imagine the object. I was as far from the proper one, as if I had been of no sex, and already young and tender, I sometimes thought of my follies, but I saw no farther. In this strange situation, my uneasy imagination took a resolution which tore me from myself, and calmed my growing sensuality. It was to contemplate

template those situations which had attracted
me in my studies, to recal them, to vary them,
to combine them, to apply them so much to
myself as to become one of the personages I
imagined, that I saw myself continually in the
most agreeable situations according to my
taste, in fine, that the fictitious situation in
which I contrived to place myself, made me
forget my real one, of which I was so discon-
tented. This fondness of imaginary objects,
and the facility of executing them, filled up
the measure of disgust for every thing around
me, and determined the inclination for solitude
which has never left me since that time. We
shall see more than once, in its place, the wild
effects of this disposition, so unsociable and
dull in appearance, but which proceed in fact
from a heart too affectionate, too amorous,
and too tender, which, for want of other beings which resemble it, is forced to be fed by
fiction. It suffices, for the present, to have
traced the origin and first cause of an inclination which has modified all my passions, and
which, containing them by themselves, has always rendered me too lazy to act, by desiring
with too much ardour.

Thus I reached sixteen, uneasy, discontent-
ed with every thing and with myself, without
relish for my trade, without the pleasures of
my age, gnawed by desires whose object I was
ignorant of, weeping without a subject of tears,
sighing without knowing for what, in fine,
caressing tenderly my chimeras, for want of
seeing something around me that equalled
them. On Sunday my companions came to

fetch

fetch me after fermon to take a part in their paftime. I would have gladly efcaped them if I could; but once beginning to play, I was more eager and went farther than the beft of them; difficult to be lead on or off. This was at all times my conftant difpofition In our walks out of the city I was always foremoft without dreaming of returning, unlefs fome one thought for me. I was caught twice; the gates were fhut before I could reach them. The next day I was treated as you may imagine, and the fecond time I was promifed fuch a reception for the third, that I refolved never to expofe myfelf to the danger of it. This third time fo much dreaded happened neverthelefs. My vigilance w s rendered ufelefs by a curfed captain called M. Minutoli, who always fhut the gate, where he was on guard, half an hour before others. I was returning with two companions. At half a league from the city I hear them found the retreat; I redouble my pace; I hear the drum beat, I run with all my might I come up out of breath, all in a fweat: my heart beats; I fee at a diftance the foldiers at their poft, I haften, I cry with a fuffocated voice. It was too late. At twenty fteps from the advanced guard, I fee the firft bridge drawn up. I tremble to fee in the air thefe terrible horns, the finifter and fatal augur of the inevitable fate this moment began for me.

In the firft tranfport of rage I threw myfelf on the glacis, and bit the earth. My companions, laughing at their accident, immediately decided on what to do. So did I, but in

a quite

a quite different manner.   On the very fpot I
fwore I would never more return to my mafter's; and the next morning, when, at the
hour of opening, they went into the city, I
bid them farewel for ever, begging them only
to acquaint privately my coufin Bernard of the
refolution I had taken, and of the place where
he might fee me once more.

On my becoming an apprentice, being more
feparated from him, I faw him lefs.   For fome
time, however, we met together on Sundays;
but infenfibly each of us took other habits, and
we faw each other but feldom.   I am perfuaded
his mother contributed much to this change.
He w s, for his part, a boy *of confequence*, I, a
pitiful apprentice; I was nothing better than
a boy from St. Gervais   Equality was no
longer to be found between us in fpite of our
birth, 'twas degrading himfelf to frequent me.
However, connections did not entirely ceafe between us; and as he was a boy naturally good,
he fometimes followed his heart in fpite of his
mother's leffons.   Having learnt my refolution,
he haftens, not to diffuade me from it, or partake
of it, but to throw in by trifling prefents fomething agreeable in my flight; for my own refources would not carry me far.   He gave me,
among other things, a little fword, which greatly pleafed me, and which I took as far as Turin,
where want caufed me to fell it; and I paffed it,
as they fay, through my body.   The more I have
reflected fince on the manner he behaved in
this critical moment, the more I am perfuaded
he followed the inftructions of his mother, and
perhaps of his father, for it is not poffible

but

but of himſelf he would have made ſome effort to retain me, or have been tempted to follow me but no. He encouraged me in my deſign rather then diſſuade me from it ; and when he ſaw me quite reſolved, he quitted me without many tears. We never more ſaw or wrote to each other, 'twas pity. He was of a character eſſentially good. we were made for each other's friendſhip.

Before I abandon myſelf to the fatality of my deſtiny, let me be permitted to turn my eyes one moment on that which naturally awaited me, had I fallen into the hands of a better maſter Nothing agreed ſo well with my humour, or was more likely to make me happy, then the quiet and obſcure condition of a good mechanic, in certain claſſes, particularly ſuch as is at Geneva that of the engravers. This art, lucrative enough for an eaſy ſubſiſtence, but not ſufficient to lead to a fortune, would have bounded my ambition for the remainder of my days, and, leaving me a decent leiſure for cultivating my moderate taſte, it had kept me in my ſphere without preſenting me any means of going beyond it. Having an imagination rich enough to ornament with its chimeras any art, powerful enough to tranſport me, in a manner, as I choſe from one to another, it ſignified little which in fact I fell into. It could not be ſo far from the place I was in, to the greateſt caſtle in Spain, but it would have been eaſy for me to have eſtabliſhed myſelf there. From whence only it followed, that the moſt ſimple condition, that which cauſed the leaſt buſtle or care, that which left the mind moſt at liberty,

was

was beſt adapted to me ; and this was abſolutely mine.   I ſhould have paſſed, in the boſom
of my religion, of my native country, of my
family and my friends, a calm and peaceable
life, ſuch as my character wanted, in the uni-
formity of a labour ſuited to my taſte, and in
a ſociety according to my heart.   I ſhould have
been a good chriſtian, a good citizen, a good
father, a kind friend, a good artiſt, a good
man. I ſhould have liked my condition, perhaps
been an honour to it ; and after having paſſed
an obſcure and ſimple life, but even and calm,
I ſhould have died peaceably on the breaſts of
my own family   Soon forgot, doubtleſs, I had
been regretted at leaſt whenever I was remembered.

Inſtead of that——what a picture am I going to draw ?   Ah ! we'll not anticipate the
miſeries of my life ; my readers will hear but
too much of the doleful ſubject.

END OF THE FIRST BOOK.

D 5   THE

THE
CONFESSIONS
OF
J. J. ROUSSEAU.

BOOK II.

AS much as the moment, when terror fuggefted the project of flight, had appeared
afflicting, fo much did that of executing it
appear charming. Still a child, leaving my
country, my parents, my fupport, my refources;
an apprenticefhip half finifhed, without knowing enough of the trade to fubfift by it ; to be
given up to the horrors of mifery, without perceiving the leaft means of getting out of it , in
the age of weaknefs and innocence, to expofe
myfelf to every temptation of vice and defpair;
feek afar off misfortune, error, fnares, flavery,
and death, under a yoke more inflexible than
that I could not bear—all this I was going to
do ; this was the perfpective I ought to have
held up. How different was that I painted to
myfelf ! The independence I thought I had
acquired was the only fentiment which ftruck
me. Free and my own mafter, I thought I
could do every thing, attain all . I had but to
launch, and I thought I could raife myfelf to

fly

fly in the air. I entered with security into the vaſt ſpace of the world, my merit was to fill it: at each ſtep I expected to find feaſting, treaſures, and adventures, friends ready to ſerve me, miſtreſſes eager to pleaſe me. I expected, on my appearance, the eyes of the univerſe to be fixed on me, not however the whole univerſe; I diſpenſed with that in ſome ſort, I did not want ſo much; a pleaſing ſociety was ſufficient without troubling my head about the reſt. My moderation inſcribed me in a narrow ſphere, but deliciouſly choſen, where I was ſure to carry the ſway. One caſtle only ſatisfied my ambition. A favourite of the lord and lady, the young lady's gallant, her brother's friend, and the neighbour's protector, I was ſatisfied; I deſired nothing more.

Awaiting this modeſt fortune, I ſauntered a few days round the city, lodging with country-folks of my acquaintance, who all received me with more kindneſs than I ſhould have found from inhabitants in the city. They welcomed me, lodged me, and fed me too well to claim the merit This could not be called receiving alms, 'twas not attended by a ſufficient air of ſuperiority.

By great travelling and running about, I went as far as Confignon, in the country of Savoy, two leagues from Geneva. The parſon's name was M. de Pontverre. This name, famous in the hiſtory of the republic, ſtruck me greatly I was curious to ſee how the deſcendants of the gentlemen of the ſpoon were formed. I went to ſee M de Pontverre. He received me well, talked of the hereſy of Geneva,

D 6   of

of the authority of our sacred mother the church, and gave me a dinner. I found very little to answer to arguments which finished in that manner, and judged that parsons who gave so good a dinner, were as good as our ministers. I was most certainly more learned than M de Pontveire, gentleman that he was; but I was too knowing a guest to be so good a theologian; and his Frangi wine, which seemed to me excellent, argued so victoriously in his favour, I should have blushed to have stopped the mouth of so kind a host. I therefore yielded, or at least I did not openly resist. To have seen all the discretion I made use of, one would have thought me false; 'tis an error. I was only courteous, that is certain. Flattery, or rather condescension, is not always a vice; it is oftener a virtue, especially in young people. The kindness we receive from a man, attaches us to him, 'tis not to impose on him we submit; 'tis not to vex him, not return evil for good. What interest had M. de Pontverre in entertaining me, treating me kindly, and wanting to convince me? None but mine. My young heart told me so. I was touched with gratitude and respect for the good-natured priest. I was sensible of my superiority; I would not trouble him in return for his hospitality. There was no hypocritical motive in this conduct: I never thought of changing my religion, and so far from contracting a familiarity with the idea, I thought of it with a horror that should have long driven it from my mind: I only meant not to vex those who flattered me with

this

this view; I meant to cultivate only their benevolence, and leave them the hopes of fuccefs
in feeming lefs armed than I really was. My
fault in that refpect refembled the coquettry of
honeft women, who fometimes, in order to gain
their point, know, without permitting or
promifing any thing, how to caufe more to be
hoped than they ever intend to perform.

Reafon, pity, and the love of order, certainly demanded, inftead of giving into
my folly, that I fhould be diffuaded from the
ruin I was running into, and by fending me
back to my friends . This is what any man,
truly virtuous, would have done. But although
M de Pontverre was a good man, he was not
a virtuous one. He was, on the contrary, a
devotee, who knew no other virtue than wor-
fhiping images, and telling his beads , a fort of
miffionary, who imagined nothing better than
writing libels againft the minifters of Geneva.
So far from thinking of fending me home
again, he took the advantage of the defire I
fhewed to leave it, by putting it out of my
power to return, even though I wifhed for it.
It was a thoufand to one ,but he was fending
me to perifh with hunger, or become a villain. He did not fee this. He faw a foul
taken from herefy, and reftored to the faith.
An honeft man or a villain, what did that import, provided I went to mafs? You muft not
imagine, however, this manner of thinking
is peculiar to Chatholics , it is that of every
dogmatical religion whofe effence is not to do,
but to believe.

God

God has called you, fays M. de Pontverre.
Go to Annecy; you will find there a good
and charitable lady, that the king's goodnefs
enables to turn fouls from the errors fhe herfelf has quitted.   He meant Madam de Warens, lately converted, whom the priefts forced,
in reality, to divide, with the blackguards
who had fold them their faith, a penfion of
two thoufand livres the king of Sardinia allowed her.   I felt myfelf extremely mortified
at having occafion to apply to a good and charitable lady.   I had no objection to their fup-
plying me with what I wanted, but not to
their beftowing charity on me, and a devotee
did not much pleafe me.   But being urged by
M. de Pontverre, and by hunger at my heels;
glad likewife to make a journey and to have a
profpect in view, I determine, though with
fome trouble, and fet off for Annecy.   I
could eafily get there in a day; but I did not
hurry, I took three   I faw no country-feat
to the right or the left, without going to feek
the adventure I was fure awaited me there.   I
dared not enter, or knock; for I was very timid:
but I fung under thofe windows which had
the beft appearance,   much furpr fed, after
having tired my lungs, to fee ne ther lad, s
nor their daughters appear, aw ed by ne
finenefs of my voice, or the grace of my fong;
as I knew fome charming ones my companions
had taught me, and which I fung moft ad-
mirably.

I at laft arrive, I fee Madam de Warens.
This period of my life has determined my
character, I could not refolve to pafs it lightly
over.

over. I was in the middle of my sixteenth year. Without being what is called a handsome fellow, I was well made for my small size I had a smart foot, good leg, an easy air, sprightly physiognomy, delicate mouth, hair and eyebrows black, small eyes rather sunk, but which threw out forcibly the fire which heated my blood. Unfortunately I knew nothing of all this; for in my life I never thought my person worth a thought, but when it was too late to make any thing of it. Thus I had, with the timidity of my age, a natural one very amiable, always uneasy for fear of displeasing. Besides, though my mind was pretty well furnished, not having seen the world, I totally failed in its manner; and my judgment, far from assisting, served only to intimidate me more, in making me sensible how little I had.

Fearing therefore my presence might prejudice me, I took a different advantage; I wrote a fine letter in the style of an orator, where tacking the phrases of books to the expression of an apprentice, I displayed all my eloquence to captivate the benevolence of Madam de Warens. I put M. de Pontverre's letter into mine, and set out for this terrible audience. I did not find Madam de Warens; I was told she was just gone to church. It was on Palm-Sunday, in the year 1728. I ran after her: I see her, I come up with her, I speak to her——I ought to remember the place; I have often since that watered it with my tears, and covered it with kisses. Why can't I surround with pillars of gold this happy spot? Why can't.

can't I perfuade the whole earth to worfhip it? Whoever is fond of honouring monuments of the falvation of the human fpecies, ought not to approach it but on their knees.

It was in a paffage behind the houfe, between a rivulet on the right hand, which feparated it from the garden, and the wall of the yard on the left, leading by a private door to the church of the Cordeliers. Juft going in at this door, Madam de Warens turns round on hearing my voice. How did I change at this fight! I expected to fee a devout grim old woman. M. de Pontverre's good woman could be nothing elfe in my opinion. I fee a face loaded with beauty, fine blue eyes full of fweetnefs, a complexion that dazzled the fight, the contour of an enchanting neck. Nothing efcaped the rapid glance of the young profelyte; for I inftantly became hers, certain that a religion preached by fuch miffionaries muft lead to heaven. She takes, fmiling, the letter I prefent with a trembling hand, opens it, runs over M. de Pontverre's, returns to mine, which fhe read through, and which fhe would have read again, had not the fervant told her the fervice was begun. So! child, fays fhe with a voice which ftartled me, you are running about the country very young; 'tis pity, indeed. And without waiting my anfwer, fhe added, Go to my houfe, tell them to give you fome breakfaft after mafs I'll come and fpeak to you

Louife-Eleonore de Warens was a young lady of La Tour de Pil, a noble and ancient family of Vevay, a city in the country of Vaud.
She

She was married very young to M. de Warens, of the house of *Loys*, eldest son of M de Villardin, of Lausanne. This marriage, which produced no children, not turning out well; M. de Warens, driven by some domestic uneasiness, took the opportunity of King Victor Amédee's presence at Evian of passing the lake, and throwing herself at the feet of this prince, thus abandoning her husband, her family, and her country, by a giddiness nearly resembling mine, which she likewise lamented at her leisure hours. The king, who loved to affect the zealous catholic, took her under his protection, gave her a pension of fifteen hundred livres of Piedmont, which was a great deal for a prince so little profuse; but perceiving, that, from this reception, he was thought amorous, he sent her to Annecy. escorted by a detachment of his guards, where, under the direction of Michel Gabriel de Bernex, titular bishop of Geneva, she made her abjuration at the convent of the Visitation.

She had been there six years when I came, and was then eight-and-twenty, being born with the century. She possessed those beauties which remain, because they are more in the physiognomy than in the features. hers was therefore in its first splendor. Her air was caressing and tender, her look extremely mild, the smile of an angel, a mouth the size of mine, her hair of an ash colour, of uncommon beauty, to which she gave a neglected turn which rendered it very smart. She was of small stature, short, and thick in the waist, though without deformity. But

it

it was impossible to see a finer face, a finer neck, more beautiful hands, or well-turned arms.

Her education was a mixture. She had, like me, lost her mother at her birth, and indifferently receiving instruction as it came, she learnt a little of her governant, a little of her father, a little of her masters, and a great deal from her lovers; particularly a M. de Tavel, who having taste and knowledge, adorned with them the person he loved. But so many different sorts of knowledge hurt each other, and the little regularity she bestowed on them prevented these several studies from extending the natural clearness of her mind. Thus, though she had some of the principles of moral and natural philosophy, she still retained the taste of her father for empirical medicine and chemistry; she prepared elixirs, tinctures, balsams, magistery, and pretended she possessed secrets. Quacks and cheats, seeing her weakness, beset her, ruined her, and consumed, amidst furnaces and drugs, her mind, her talents, and her charms, which might have been the delight of the noblest society.

But although these vile knaves abused her education, ill directed, to darken the lights of her reason, her excellent heart was proof, and remained always the same : her amiable and mild character, her feelings for misfortunes, her unbounded goodness, her sprightly humour, open and free, never changed, not even at the approach of age. plunged into indigence, ills, and divers calamities, the serenity

nity of her noble foul preferved, to the laft, all the chearfulnefs of her happy days.

Her errors proceeded from a fund of inexhauftible activity, which inceffantly demanded employment. It was not the intrigues of women fhe wanted, 'twas planning and directing new undertakings. She was born for great affairs. Madam de Longueville, in her place, would have been a mere pretender; fhe, in Madam de Longueville's place, had governed the ftate. Her talents were mifplaced, and that which would have raifed her to honour in a more exalted ftation, ruined her in that fhe lived. In things within her reach fhe always drew her plan in her mind, and always comprehended her object. This was the caufe, that, by employing means proportioned to her view, more than to her ftrength, fhe mifcarried by others faults; and, her plan failing, fhe was ruined, where others would hardly have loft any thing. This inclination for bufinefs, which brought on her fo many evils, was of great fervice to her in her monaftic afylum, in preventing her from paffing the remainder of her days there as fhe intended. The uniform and fimple life of a nun, the filly goffiping of their parlour, could never flatter a mind always in motion, which, forming each day new fyftems, wanted liberty to expand itfelf The good bifhop de Bernex, with lefs wit than Francis of Sales, refembled him in many points; and Madam de Warens, whom he called his child, and who refembled Madam de Chantal in many others, might have refembled her in her retirement, had not her tafte
diverted

diverted her from the laziness of a convent.
It was not want of zeal that prevented this
amiable woman from giving herself up to
the trifling formalities of devotion which seemed necessary to a new convert under the direction of a prelate. Whatever was her motive for changing her religion, she was sincere
in that she had embraced. She might repent
for having committed the fault, but she did
not desire to return to her former profession.
She not only died a good catholic, she lived
one in good earnest, and I dare affirm, I who
think I have read the bottom of her soul, that
it was solely aversion to grimace that she did
not act the devotee in public. She had a piety
too solid to affect devotion. But this is not
the place to enlarge on her principles, I shall
find other occasions to speak of them

Let those who deny the sympathy of hearts
explain, if they can, how, on the first interview, the first word, the first look, Madam
de Warens inspired me, not only with the
liveliest passion, but a perfect confidence,
which was always retained. Suppose what I
felt for her was really love; which would,
however, appear very doubtful to those who
will follow the history of our amity, why
was this passion accompanied from its birth
with sentiments it least inspires, the tranquillity of the heart, calmness, serenity, security,
assurance—How in approaching, for the first
time, an amiable, polite, and dazzling woman, a lady in a superior situation to mine,
and such as I had never access to before, her
on whom depended my destiny, in some measure,

sure, by the interest, more or less, she might take in it, how, I say, with all this, do I find myself as free, as easy, as if perfectly sure of pleasing her? Why had not I a moment's perplexity, timidity, or constraint? Naturally bashful and discountenanced, having seen nothing, why did I take the first day, the first instant, the freedom of manner, the tender language, the familiar style, I had ten years afterwards, when the closest intimacy had rendered them natural to me? Do we feel love, I don't say without desires, for I had them, but without uneasiness, without jealousy? Would not one, at least, know from the object we love, whether we are loved? That is a question which no more came into my mind ever once to ask her, than to ask whether I was loved by myself, nor was she ever more curious with me. There certainly was something very singular in my feelings for this charming woman, and you will find, by the sequel, extravagances you do not expect.

The question was what was to be done with me, and to talk of it more at leisure she kept me to dinner. This was the first meal of my life where I wanted appetite, and her woman, who waited at table, said too, I was the first traveller of my age and of my sort she had seen wanting it. This remark, which did not hurt me in the mind of her mistress, fell a little hard on a great fellow who dined with us, and devoured to his own share a meal sufficient for six people. As to me, I was in an extacy that did not permit me to eat. My heart
was

was fed by a feeling quite new, which engrossed my whole being; it left me no knowledge for other functions.

Madam de Warens wanted to know the particulars of my little history: I once more found, in telling it her, all the heat I had lost at my master's. The more I engaged this excellent soul in my favour, the more she complained of the fate to which I was going to expose myself. Her tender compassion appeared in her mien, in her looks, and in her gesture. She dared not exhort me to return to Geneva. In her situation 'twas a crime of high treason against catholicism, and she was not ignorant how much she was watched, and how her conversation was weighed. But she spoke in so touching a tone of my father's affliction, you might plainly see she would have approved of my going to console him. She did not know how much, without thinking on't, she pleaded against herself. Besides, my resolution was taken, as I think I told her: the more I found her eloquent and persuasive, and the more her discourse reached my heart, the less I could resolve to separate from her. I saw that to return to Geneva was raising an almost insurmountable barrier between her and me, without returning in the steps I had taken, and to which it was as well to keep at once. I therefore kept to it Madam de Warens, seeing her endeavours fruitless, did not proceed so as to expose herself. but, says she, with a look of compassion, Poor little fellow, thou must go where God calls thee; but when thou art grown up, thou wilt remember me. I fancy
she

she did not think this prediction would be so cruelly accomplished

The whole difficulty still remained: How subsist so young from my own country? Scarcely reached half my apprenticeship, I was far from knowing my trade. Had I known it, I could not live by it at Savoy, a country too poor for arts. The great fellow who dined for us, obliged to make a pause to relieve his jaws, gave an advice which he said came from heaven, but which, to judge by its effects, came rather from the contrary place. It was that I should go to Turin, where, in an hospital, founded for the instruction of the catechumens, I should have, said he, temporal and spiritual food, until, belonging to the church, I should find, by the charity of good people, a place that would suit me. As to the expences of the journey, his Highness my Lord Bishop will not be backward, when Madam proposes this holy work, in providing in a charitable manner for it; and Madam the Baroness, who is so charitable, said he, leaning over his plate, will with earnestness, certainly, contribute likewise.

I thought all these charities very afflicting: my heart was full; I said nothing, and Madam de Warens, without catching at this project with the ardour it was offered, contented herself with saying every one ought to contribute to good according to their abilities, and that she would speak of it to his Lordship: but this devil of a man, who dreaded she would not speak to his wishes, and who had a trifling interest in the business, ran and acquainted the

the almoners, and so well instructed these good-natured priests, that when Madam de Warens, who dreaded the journey, would have spoken of it to the Bishop, she found it was an affair settled, and he instantly gave her the money destined for my little viaticum. She dared not ask my stay; I was approaching the age when a woman like her could not decently want to keep a young man with her.

My journey being thus regulated by those who were so careful of me, I was obliged to submit, and I did it even without much repugnance. Although Turin was farther than Geneva, I imagined, that, being the capital, it had relation with Annecy more than with a city which was foreign to its state and religion. besides, departing to obey Madam de Warens, I looked on myself as still living under her direction; 'twas more than living in her neighbourhood In fine, the idea of a great journey flattered my wandering fancy, which already began to shew itself It seemed a fine thing to me to pass the mountains at my age, and to raise myself above my companions by the whole height of the Alps. To see the world is an allurement a Genevan rarely resists, I therefore gave my consent. My great fellow was to set off within two days with his wife; I was intrusted and recommended to them, as was likewise my purse, which was increased by Madam de Warens. she likewise secretly gave me a little stock, to which she added ample instructions, and we set off on Ash-Wednesday.

The

The day after I left Annecy, my father, who had traced me, arrived, with a M. Rival, his friend, a watchmaker like himself, a man of sense, of letters even, who wrote verse better than La Motte, and spoke almost as well as he; nay more, he was a perfectly honest man, but whose misplaced learning only served to make his son an actor.

These gentlemen saw Madam de Warens, and contented themselves with lamenting my fate, with her, instead of following and over-taking me, which they might have done with ease, being on horseback and I on foot. The same thing happened with my uncle Bernard. He came as far as Confignon, and from thence, knowing I was at Annecy, he returned to Geneva. It seemed my relations conspired with my stars to give me up to the destiny which awaited me. My brother was lost by a like negligence, and so thoroughly lost they never knew what became of him.

My father was not only a man of honour; he was a man of great probity, and had one of those generous souls which produce shining virtues. Besides, he was a good father, particularly to me. He loved me very tenderly, but he also loved pleasure, and other inclinations had a little cooled paternal affection since I lived a great distance from him. He married again at Nion; and although his wife was not of an age to give me brothers, she had relations: that made another family, he had other objects, other connections, which did not often recal me to his memory. My father was growing old without any support for old-age. My brother and

I had a trifling legacy by my mother, the interest of which was for my father during our
absence. The idea did not strike him directly,
or prevent him from doing his duty; but it
acted sullenly without his perceiving it, and
sometimes slackened his zeal, which he had
carried farther without it. This is, I think, the
reason, that, once traced as far as Annecy, he
did not follow me quite to Chambery, where
he was morally sure to come up with me.
This is also the reason, that, going often to
see him since my flight, he always shewed
me the caresses of a father, but without great
efforts to detain me.

This conduct of a father, whose tenderness
and virtue I was so well acquainted with,
has caused me to make reflections on myself,
which have not a little contributed to keep my
heart sound. I drew from it this great maxim
of morality, the only one perhaps in practical
use, to shun those situations which put our
duty in opposition with our interests, and which
shew us our good in the misfortunes of others;
and that in such situations, however sincere a
love for virtue we bear, we weaken sooner or
later without perceiving it, and become unjust
and wicked in fact, without ceasing to be just
and innocent at the heart.

This maxim, strongly inprinted on my heart,
and put in practice in all my conduct, though
a little late, is one of those which have given
me the most whimsical and foolish appearance,
not only among the public, but more particularly among my acquaintance. I have been
charged with being original, and not doing
like

like others. In fact, I thought little of doing either like others or otherwise than they did. I sincerely desired to do what was right. I avoided, as much as possible, those situations which procured me an interest contrary to that of another man, and consequently a secret, though involuntary desire of hurting that man.

Two years ago, my Lord Maréchal would have put me down in his will. I opposed it with all my power. I wrote him word I would not for the world know I was in any man's will, and much less in his. He complied; at present he offers me an annuity, I don't oppose it. They'll say I find my account in this change: that may be. But, oh! my benefactor, my father, if I have the misfortune to survive you, I know that in losing you I lose every thing, and that I shall not get by it.

This is, according to me, sound philosophy, the only one that truly suits the human heart. I am every day more penetrated with its great solidity, and have resumed it in different manners in my late works: but the public, who are frivolous, have not been able to remark it. If I survive the completion of this undertaking long enough to begin another, I propose giving, in a continuation of Emilius, an example so charming and so striking of this same maxim, that my readers shall be forced to observe it. But here are reflections enough for a traveller; it is time to go on my journey.

I made it more agreeable than might be expected, and my clown was not so morose as he appeared. He was a man of a middle age, wore his grisly black hair cued, a grenadier's air, strong voice, gay enough, a good walker, a better eater, and who was of all trades, for want of knowing any one. He proposed, I think, to establish at Annecy I don't know what manufactory. Madam de Warens did not fail to give into the project, and it was to get it approved by the minister, he undertook, expences which were well repaid him, the journey to Turin. This man had the talent of intrigue in pushing himself always amongst the priests, and, affecting a readiness to serve them, he had learnt at their school a certain devout jargon which he incessantly made use of, setting himself up as a great preacher. He also knew a Latin passage of the Bible, and it was as if he had known a thousand; for he repeated it a thousand times a day. but rarely in want of money, when he knew of any in others purses: more cunning, however, than knavish, and dealing out, in the tone of a mountebank, his paltry sermon, he resembled the hermit Peter preaching his crusade, with his sword by his side.

As to Madam Sabran, his wife, she was a good-natured woman enough, quieter by day than by night. As I always lay in their chamber, her noisy watchings often awoke me, and would have awakened me much more, had I known the cause: but I did not even suspect it, I was in the chapter of dulness, which left to nature only the whole care of my instruction.

I got on gaily with my pious guide and his bucksome companion. No accident troubled our journey, I was in the most happy situa-

tion

tion of body and mind I ever was in my days. Young, vigorous, full of health, security, and confidence in myself and others, I was in that short but precious moment of life, when its expansive plenitude extends in a manner our being over all our sensations, and embellishes, in our eyes, all nature with the charms of our existence. My sweet uneasiness had an object which rendered it less wandering, and fixed my imagination I looked on myself as the work, the pupil, the friend, almost the lover of Madam de Warens. The obliging things she said to me, the little caresses she gave me, the tender concern she seemed to have for me, her charming looks, which appeared to me full of love, because they inspired me with love; all this fed my ideas during the way, and made me rave deliciously. No fear, no doubt of my fate, troubled these dreams. To send me to Turin was, in my opinion, to give me life, to place me agreeably. I had no apprehension about myself; others had taken those cares on them. Thus I walked on lightly, eased of that weight · youthful desires, enchanting wishes, brilliant projects, filled my thoughts. Every object I saw seemed to warrant my approaching felicity. In the houses I imagined rural feastings, in the meadows wanton games, along the river baths, walks, and fish, on the trees delicious fruit, under their shade voluptuous meetings, on the mountains tubs of milk and cream, a charming laziness, peace, simplicity, and the pleasure of going one don't know where. In fine, nothing struck my sight without carrying to my heart

some

some inticement to enjoyment. The grandeur, the variety, the real beauty of the prospect, rendered these delights worthy of my reason. Vanity too threw in its mite. So young and go to Italy, already to have seen so much country, to follow Hannibal across the mountains, seemed a glory beyond my age. Add to all this, frequent and good repose, a good appetite and plenty to satisfy it; for faith it was not worth while to let me want, and at the table of M. Sabran what I eat could not be missed.

I don't recollect to have had, in the whole course of my life, an interval more perfectly exempt from cares and trouble, than the seven or eight days we took to make this journey; for the pace of Madam Sabran, by which ours was regulated, made it no more than a long walk. This remembrance has left me a lively relish for every thing which resembles it, particularly for mountains and journeys on foot. I journeyed on foot in my best days only, and always with delight. Very soon business, luggage to carry, forced me to act the gentleman and take a carriage · care, embarasment, and constraint, got in with me, and from that time, instead of feeling, as I used to do in my former journeys, nothing but the pleasure of going, I felt nothing so much as the desire of getting to the end. I long sought at Paris for two companions of the same turn as myself, who would devote fifty guineas from their pockets, and a twelvemonth's time, to make together, and on foot, the tour of Italy, without any other incumbrance than a young fellow
low

low to carry a bag for our night-shirts. Many
offered, much pleased in appearance with the
project; but at bottom, taking the whole as a
mere castle in the air, which we talk over in
conversation without intending to execute it
in fact.   I remember, that, speaking with delight of this project to Diderot and Grimm,
I at last gave them a fancy to it.   I once
thought it a thing done; but the whole ended in making a journey on paper, in which
Grimm found nothing so pleasing as to make
Diderot do a great many impious actions, and
to thrust me in the Inquisition in his place.

My regret at arriving so soon at Turin, was
alleviated by the pleasure of seeing a great
city, and by the hope of soon figuring there
in a manner worthy of me, for the fumes of
ambition had already reached my head   I
already regarded myself as much above the
condition of an apprentice; I was far from
foreseeing that in a short time I should be
much below it.

Before I proceed farther, I ought to make
to the reader my excuse or justification, as
well for the trifling narrations I have just entered into, as for those I may enter into afterwards, and which have nothing engaging
in his eyes.   In the work I have undertaken
of exposing myself entirely to the public, nothing of myself must remain obscure or hid-
den, I must keep myself incessantly under
their eye, that they may follow me, through
all the wanderings of my heart, into every
recess of my life, for fear lest, finding in
my relation the least void, the least gap,

it fhould be faid, What was he doing all that time? or I fhould be accufed of not having told all. I give fcope enough to the malignity of men, by my relation, without giving ftill more by my filence.

My little ftock was gone; I had been babbling, and my indifcretion was not to my conductors an entire lofs. Madam Sabran found means to get from me even a little ribband, embroidered with filver, which Madam de Warens had given me for my little fword, which I regretted more than all the reft the fword had alfo remained with them, had I been lefs obftinate. They faithfully defrayed my expences on the journey, but had left me nothing. I arrive at Turin without cloaths, without money, and without linnen; and leaving wholly to my fole merit all the honour of the fortune I was going to make.

I had letters, I carried them, and was immediately led to the Hofpital of the Catechumens, to be inftructed in a religion for which they fold me my fubfiftence. In going an I faw a large door with iron bars, which when I had paffed was double-locked on my heels. This beginning appeared to me more impofing than agreeable, and began to fet me thinking, when I was conducted to a prety large room. All the furniture that was there was a wooden altar, with a large crucifix on it, at the bottom of the room, and around it, four or five chairs, alfo of wood, which appeared to have been rubbed with wax, but which fhone only from continual rubbing. In this affembly-hall were four or five frightful

ban-

banditti, my companions of inftruction, but which feemed rather the devil s body-guard than candidates for the kingdom of God. Two of thefe villains were Efclavonians, who called themfelves Jews or Moors, and who, as they owned to me, paffed their time in running over Spain and Italy embracing Chriftianity, and being baptized wherever the produce was worth the labour. Another door of iron was opened, which divided in two a large balcony that gave into the court. By this door entered our fifters the catechumens, who like me were going to be regenerated, not by baptifm, but by a folemn abjuration They were the greateft fluts and the naftieft ftreet-walkers that ever beftunk the flock of our Lord. One only feemed pretty and engaging enough She was nearly of my age, perhaps a year or two older. She had roguifh eyes, which now and then met mine. That gave me fome defire to be acquainted with her; but during almoft two months fhe remained in this houfe, where fhe had already been three, it was impoffible to accoft her. So much was fhe recommended to our old jailor's wife, and watched by the holy miffionary, who laboured for her converfion with more zeal than diligence She muft have been extremely ftupid, though fhe did not appear fo, for never was fo long an inftruction. The holy man never found her in a ftate to abjure, but fhe grew weary of her cloifter, and faid fhe would go out chriftian or not. They were obliged to take her at the word while fhe yet confented to become one, for fear fhe fhould grow refractory, and hear no more of it.

The

The little community was affembled in honour of the new comer. They made us a fhort exhortation; to me, to engage me to correfpond with the favour God beftowed on me; to the others, to invite them to grant me their prayers, and edify me by their example. This done, our virgins being returned to their cloifter, I had time to contemplate, quite at my cafe, that wherein I found myfelf.

The next morning we were again affembled for inftruction : it was then I began to reflect, for the firft time, on the ftep I was about to take, and on the proceedings which brought me there.

I have faid, I repeat, and fhall repeat, perhaps, a thing whereof I am every day more perfuaded; which is, that, if a child ever received an education reafonable and found, it was I Born of a family whofe morals diftinguifhed it from the vulgar, I received none but leffons of prudence, and examples of honour from all my relations. My father, though a man of pleafure, had not only great honour, but a deal of religion. Gallant in the world, and a chriftian in the interior, he fuggefted to me thofe fentiments with which he was penetrated. Of my three aunts, all prudent and virtuous, the two eldeft were devotees; the third, a girl at the fame time full of grace, wit, and fenfe, was perhaps more fo than them, though with lefs oftentation. From the bofom of this eftimable family, I went to M. Lambercier's, who, though of the church and a preacher, believed inwardly, and

acted

acted almost as well as he said.   His sister and
himself cultivated, by gentle and judicious
instruction, the principles of piety they found
in my heart.   These worthy people employed,
to that end, means so apt, so discreet, and so
reasonable, that, far from wearying me with
their sermon, I never left it without being in-
ternally touched, and making resolutions to
live well, in which, by seriously thinking on it,
I rarely failed.   At my aunt Bernard's, devotion was a little more tiresome, because she
made a science of it.   At my master's, I
thought little more of it, without, however,
thinking differently.   I found no young people to pervert me.   I became a blackguard,
but not a libertine.

I had then as much religion as a child of
the age I was of could have.   I had even more,
for why should I now disguise my thoughts?
My childhood was not that of a child   I felt,
I thought always as a man.   'Twas only in
growing up I returned to the ordinary class;
at my birth I left it.   I shall be laughed at
thus to give myself out for a prodigy.   Be it
so, but when they have laughed heartily, let
them find a child that at six years old a romance affects, moves, and transports, to a
degree of weeping showers of tears, I shall
then see my ridiculous vanity, and will agree
I am wrong.

Thus, when I said we should not converse
with children on religion, if we wished they
might one day have any, and that they were
incapable of knowing God, even after our
manner; I drew my sentiment from my obser-

L 6   vations,

vations, not from my own experience. I
knew it was not conclusive to others. Find
J. J. Rousseaus at six years old, and talk to
them on God at seven, I will be answerable
you run no hazard

It is understood, I suppose, that for a child,
or even a man, to have religion, is to follow
that he was born in. Sometimes you take
from it; rarely add to it dogmatical faith is
the fruit of education. Besides this common
principle which tied me to the religion of my
forefathers, I had the peculiar aversion of
our city for catholicism, which we were taught
was dreadful idolatry, and whose clergy were
painted in the blackest colours. This sentiment was carried so far in me, that, at the
beginning, I never glanced towards the in-
side of a church, never met a priest in his
surplice, never heard the bell of a procession,
without shaking with terror and affright,
which soon left me in cities, but has returned
in the country parishes that had more re-
semblance to those where I first experienced
it. It is true, this impression was singularly
contrasted by the remembrance of the caresses
which the priests of the environs of Geneva
bestow on the children of the city. At the
same time the hand-bell for the viaticum made
me afraid, the bells for mass or vespers reminded me of a breakfast, a collation, fresh
butter, fruits, or milk. The good dinner at
M. de Pontverre's still produced a great effect. Thus was I easily turned from those
thoughts. Considering popery only as it related to amusement or guttling, I accommo-
dated

dated myself, without trouble, to the idea of living in it: but that of solemnly entering into it, never presented itself to me but in a passing manner, and in a very distant futurity. At this time there was no means of changing· I saw, with the most violent horror, the sort of engagement I had made, and its inevitable consequence. The future Neophytes I had around me were not adapted to support my courage by their example; I could not dissimulate that the holy deed I was going to perform was, at the bottom, but the action of a cut-throat. Though still young, I saw, that, whatever religion was the true one, I was going to sell mine; and that, though I should even chuse well, I was going, from the bottom of my heart, to lie to the Holy Ghost, and merit the contempt of mankind. The more I thought on it, the more I despised myself, I trembled at the fate that had led me there, as if this fate was not my own doing. Sometimes these reflections were so powerful, that, if I had seen the door open one instant, I should certainly have gone out of it; but it was not possible, and this resolution did not hold, neither, very strong.

Too many secret desires combatted it not to vanquish. Besides, the obstinacy of the design formed not to return to Geneva, the shame, and even the difficulty of repassing the mountains, the trouble at seeing myself far from my country, and without a friend, without resources, all these things concurred to make me regard, as a late repentance, the remorse of conscience: I affected to reproach
myself

myfelf of what I had done, to excufe that I was going to do. In aggravating the faults of the paft, I looked on future ones as their neceffary effect. I did not fay to myfelf, Nothing is yet done, and you can be innocent if you will; but I faid, Lament the crime of which you have rendered yourfelf culpable, and of which you have made it neceffary to fill up the meafure.

In fact, what rare magnanimity of foul muft I not have had, at my age, to revoke all that, till that moment, I had promifed or left to hope, to break the chains I had given myfelf, to declare with intrepidity that I would remain in the religion of my forefathers, at the rifk of all that might happen! This vigour was not of my age, and there is little probability of its having had a happy iffue. Things were too far advanced to be recalled, and the more my refiftance had been great, the more, by fome manner or other, they had made it a merit to furmount it.

The fophifm which ruined me is that of the greateft part of mankind, who complain of want of power, when it is too late to make ufe of it. Virtue is dearly bought by our own fault; if we were always prudent, we fhould feldom have occafion of virtue. But inclinations which might be eafily furmounted, drag us without refiftance; we yield to light temptations whofe danger we defpife. Infenfibly we fall into perilous fituations from which we might eafily have preferved ourfelves, but from which we cannot extricate ourfelves without heroic efforts which affright us;

us; so we fall at last into the abyss, in saying to
God, Why hast thou made us so weak? But,
in spite of us, he replies by our conscience,
I made you too weak to get out of the gulf,
because I made you strong enough not to fall
into it.

I did not precisely take the resolution of
becoming a catholic; but seeing the time was
not very nigh, I took time to accustom myself
to the idea, and thought that in the mean
while some unforeseen event might deliver me
from my embarrasment. In order to gain time,
I resolved to make the best defence possible.
Very soon my vanity dispensed me from thinking of my resoluti.n; and whenever I perceived I sometimes puzzled those who would
instruct me, nothing more was wanting than
to try entirely to overthrow them. I even
applied in this undertaking a zeal very ridiculous; for while they were at work on me,
I wanted to work on them. I honestly thought
they wanted no more than conviction to become protestants.

They did not, therefore, find in me that
facility they expected, neither on the side of
knowledge or will. Protestants are, in general, better instructed than catholics. It cannot be otherwise. the doctrine of the one ex-
acts discussion, that of the other submission.
A catholic must adopt the decision they give
him, a protestant must learn to decide for himself. They knew that, but they did not expect, either from my condition or my age,
much difficulty to people exercised as they
were. Besides, I had not yet received my
first

firſt communion, or received thoſe inſtructions
which relate to it: they knew that too, but
they did not know, that, in its ſtead, I had
been well inſtructed at M Lambercier's , and
that, moreover, I had by me a little magazine,
very troubleſome to theſe gentlemen, in the
hiſtory of the church and of the empire, which
I had learnt almoſt by heart at my father's,
and ſince that almoſt forgot, but which returned again to my memory, as the diſpute grew
warmer.

An old little prieſt, but pretty venerable,
held with us, in common, the firſt conference.
This conference was, to my companions, a
catechiſm rather than a controverſy , he had
more trouble in inſtructing, than reſolving
their objections.   It was not the ſame with
me.   When my turn came, I ſtopped him at
every point, I did not ſpare him one difficulty
I could give him.   This rendered the conference very long, and very tireſome to the
aſſiſtants.   My old prieſt talked much, exerted
himſelf, ran to his books, and got out of the
hobble by ſaying he did not underſtand French
enough.   The next day, for fear my indiſcreet
objections ſhould hurt my companions, they
put me in a ſeparate room with another prieſt,
much younger, a good talker, that is to ſay,
dealing out long phraſes, and proud of himſelf, if ever doctor was.   I did not, however,
ſuffer myſelf to be too much brought under by
his impoſing countenance, and finding, after
all, that I made my way, I began to anſwer
him with a tolerable aſſurance, and to maul
him, on right and left, as well as I could.
                                                          He

He thought to knock me down with Saint Augustin, Saint Gregory, and the rest of the fathers, but he found, with an incredible surprise, I could handle all these fathers almost as nimbly as he could not that I ever read them, or he either perhaps; but I retained many passages taken from my *Le Sueur*; and whenever he cited one, without disputing on the citation, I parried it by another from the same father, and which, often, greatly puzzled him He got the better, however, at last, for two reasons. one was, he was above me; and seeing myself, in a manner, at his mercy, being so young, I rightly judged I should not drive him to a non-plus; for I plainly saw the little old priest was not well satisfied with my erudition or me.   The other reason was, the young one had studied, and I had not. That gave him, in his manner of argument, a method I could not follow; and whenever he found himself unable to answer an unexpected objection, he put it off till the next day, pretending I left the present subject. Sometimes he rejected even all my citations, maintaining they were false, and, offering to fetch the book, defied me to find them.   He knew he ran no great hazard, and that, with all my borrowed learning, I was too little exercised in the handling books, and not Latinist enough, to find a passage in a large volume, even though I was assured it was there. I suspect him likewise of having made use of the perfidy of which he accused the ministers, and having sometimes forged passages to extricate himself from an objection which troubled him.

But,

But, at laſt, the reſidence of the hoſpital becoming every day more diſagreeable, and perceiving to get out of it but one way, I was as eager to take it as I had been in endeavouring to retard it.

The two Africans had been baptized with great ceremony, dreſſed in white from head to foot, to repreſent the candour of their regenerated ſoul. My turn came a month afterwards, for all that time was neceſſary, that my directors might have the honour of a difficult converſion, and all their tenets were called over before me, to triumph over my new docility

In fine, ſufficiently inſtructed and ſufficiently diſpoſed to the will of my new maſters, I was led proceſſionally to the metropolitan church of St. John, to make a ſolemn abjuration, and receive the addition of baptiſm, though they did not re-baptize me in reality: but as the ceremony is nearly the ſame, it ſerves to perſuade the people proteſtants are not chriſtians. I was cloathed in a kind of grey gown, and a white ſurtout coat, devoted to theſe occaſions. Two men carried before and behind copper baſons, on which they ſtruck a key, where every one put alms according to his devotion, or the concern he had for the welfare of the new convert In fact, nothing of catholic pageantry was omitted to render the ſolemnity more edifying to the public, and more humiliating to me. The white coat only might have been uſeful to me, which they did not give me as to a Moor, ſince I had not the honour of being a jew.

This

This was not all. I muft afterwards go
to the Inquifition, to receive abfolution for
the crime of herefy, and return to the bofom
of the church, with the fame ceremony to
which Henry IV. was fubjected by his Ambaffador. The countenance and manner of
the right reverend father Inquifitor was not
of the fort to diminifh the fecret terror which
had feized me on entering this houfe. After
feveral queftions on my faith, on my condition, and on my family, he afked me bluntly
if my mother was damned. My confternation
repreffed the firft motions of my indignation ;
I contented myfelf with replying, I would
hope fhe was not, and that God might have
enlightened her at her laft hour The monk
was filent ; but his four look did not appear
to me a fign of approbation.

All this got through, at the moment I expected to be, at laft, placed according to my
wifhes, they turned me out of doors with fomething more than twenty livres in fmall money,
which the gathering produced. They recommended to me to live a good chriftian, be
faithful to grace ; they wifhed me good luck,
fhut the door on me, and every one difappeared.

Thus, in an inftant, were all my grand ex-
pectations at an end, and nothing remained
of the felfifh fteps I had taken, but the remembrance of having been, at once, an
apoftate and a dupe. It is eafy to guefs what
a fudden revolution muft have been caufed
in my ideas, when, from my fhining projects
of fortune, I faw myfelf defcend to the com-

pletest misery, and that, after deliberating, in the morning, on the choice of the palace I should inhabit, I saw myself, at night, reduced to lie in the street. You would think I began to give myself up to a despair, so much the more cruel, as the sorrow for my faults must have been heightened by a conviction that my misfortunes were of my own seeking—Not a bit of all that. I had been, for the first time, in my days, shut up more than two months. The first sentiment that struck me was that of the liberty I recovered. After a long slavery, again become master of myself and my actions, I saw myself in a great city abounding in resources, full of people of quality, whereof my talents and merit could not fail to make me welcome as soon as they heard of me. I had, besides, time to wait, and twenty livres I had in my pocket seemed a treasure which would never be exhausted. I could dispose of it at my fancy, without rendering account to any one. It was the first time I found myself so rich. Far from falling into despondency and tears, I only changed my hopes; and self-love lost nothing by it. Never did I feel so much confidence and security: I thought my fortune already made; and that it was noble, the obligation was to myself alone.

The first thing I did was satisfying my curiosity in running all over the city, though it should be as an act of my liberty I went to see them mount guard, the military instruments pleased me much. I followed processions; I liked the irregular music of the priests.

I went

I went to see the king's palace . I approached
it with dread , but seeing other people go in,
I did like them ; they let me go in : perhaps
I was indebted for this favour to the little
bundle under my arm.   Be that as it may, I
conceived a great opinion of myself in being
in the palace , I already looked on myself as
almoft an inhabitant there.   At length, by
running backwards and forwards, I grew tired;
I was hungry : it was hot ; I go to a milk-
fhop   they brought me some curds and
milk, and with two flices of the charming
Piedmont bread, which I prefer to any other,
I made, for five or six fous, one of the beft
dinners I ever made in my life.

It was time to feek a lodging.   As I already
knew enough of the Piedmont tongue to make
myfelf underftood, there was no great difficulty in finding one ; and I had the prudence
to chufe it more adapted to my purfe than
my tafte.   I was told of a foldier's wife, in the
Po-ftreet, who received fervants out of place,
at one fous per night.   I found there, empty,
a bed, and took poff-ffion of it.   She was young,
and juft married, though fhe already had five
or fix children.   We all flept in the fame
room, mother, children, and lodgers , and it
continued in this manner whilft I remained
with her.   As for the reft, fhe was a good-
natured woman, fwearing like a carter, breafts
always open, and cap off, but a feeling heart,
officious, and inclined to ferve me, and was
even ufeful to me.

I fpent feveral days in giving myfelf up
wholly to the pleafure of independence and
curiofity.

curiosity. I went wandering within and without the city, fereting and visiting every thing which seemed curious or new, and every thing was so for a young lad coming from his nest, and had never seen the capital. I was very exact in paying my court, and regularly assisting every morning at the king's mass. I thought it fine to be in the same chapel with this prince and his retinue; but my passion for music, which began to shew itself, had more share in my assiduity than the splendor of the court, which, soon seen and always the same, did not strike me long. The King of Sardinia had, at that time, the best symphony in Europe. Somis, Des Jardins, and les Bezuzzi, shone alternately. Less would have been sufficient to draw a young fellow, that the sound of the least instrument, provided it was just, transported with gladness. Besides, I had only a stupid admiration for magnificence, which strikes the sight, without desire. The only thing I thought of in all the pomp of the court, was to find a young princess there who deserved my respect, and with whom I could act a romance

I was not far from beginning one in a situation less brilliant; but where, had I brought it to a conclusion, I had found pleasures a thousand times more delicious.

Though I lived with great œconomy, my purse insensibly grew lighter. This œconomy, however, was less the effect of prudence than a simplicity of taste, which even at this day the use of plentiful tables has not altered. I did not know, or do not yet know, a better

feast

feaſt than a country meal With milk-diet, eggs, herbs, cheeſe, brown bread, and tolerable wine, you are ſure to regale me well ; a good appetite will do the reſt, if a ſteward and the ſervants around me do not ſatiate me with their impertinent aſpect. I then made a much better meal at the expence of ſix or ſeven ſous, than I have ſince made for ſix or ſeven livres. I was therefore ſober, for want of a temptation to be otherwiſe. I am ſtill to blame to call it ſobriety ; for I employed all poſſible ſenſuality. My pears, my cheeſe, my bread, and a few glaſſes of Montſerrat wine, that you might cut with a knife, rendered me the happieſt of gluttons. But ſtill, with all that, it was poſſible to ſee the end of twenty livres ; this I from day to day more ſenſibly perceived, and, in ſpite of the giddineſs of my age, my uneaſineſs for hereafter was inclining to terror. Of all my caſtles in the air, there only remained that of ſeeking an occupation I could live by, and that was not very eaſily realized. I thought of my old trade, but knew not enough of it to work with a maſter; beſides, maſters don't abound at Turin. I therefore took a reſolution of offering, from ſhop to ſhop, to engrave a cypher, or coats of arms, on plates or diſhes, hoping to tempt them by cheapneſs, in ſubmitting to their diſcretion. This expedient was not very happy. I was almoſt every where denied, and what I got to do was ſo trifling, I could hardly earn a meal. One day, however, paſſing pretty early in the Contranova, I ſaw, through the windows of a counter, a young tradeſwoman, ſo

graceful

graceful and of fo attractive a countenance,
that, in fpite of my timidity towards ladies, I
did not hefitate to go in and offer my talent.
She did not difcourage me, made me fit down,
tell her my little ftory, pitied me, told me to
be of good cheer, and that good chriftians
would never abandon me : then, while fhe
fent for the tools I wanted to a jeweller's of the
neighbourhood, fhe went into the kitchen, and
herfelf brought me fome breakfaft.   This beginning feemed to promife well enough, the
end did not contradict it.   She feemed fatisfied
with my little labours, much more with my
prattle, when I had a little collected myfelf
for fhe was brilliant and dreffy, and, in fpite
of her graceful countenance, this luftre had
impofed on me.   But her reception full of
good-nature, her compaffionate tone, her gentle
and careffing manner, foon brought me to
myfelf.   I faw I fucceeded, and that made me
fucceed the more, but though an Italian, and
too pretty not to be a little of the coquette,
fhe was neverthelefs fo modeft, and I fo timid,
that it was difficult to bring our acquaintance
to any good.   They did not give us time to
finifh the adventure. I recollect with a greater
pleafure only the fhort moments I paffed with
her, and I can fay I there tafted in their prime
the fofteft and the pureft pleafures of love.

She was a brown girl, extremely fmart, but
whofe natural goodnefs, painted in her pretty
face, rendered her vivacity touching. Her name
was Madam Bafile.   Her hufband, older than
fhe was, and tolerably jealous, left her during
his abfence under the care of a clerk, too

difagreeable

difagreeable to be dangerous, but who neverthelefs had pretenfions which he rarely fhewed
but by ill-humour. He fhewed me a great
deal, though I was fond of hearing him play
the flute, which he did pretty well. This
fecond Ægiftus always grumbled whenever he
faw me go into his lady's room : he treated me
with a difdain which fhe heartily returned him.
She feemed as if fhe took a pleafure in tormenting him, by careffing me in his prefence, and
this fort of vengeance, though much to my wifh,
would have been much more fo in a tête-à-tête.
But fhe did not carry it quite fo far, or, rather,
it was not in the fame manner. Whether fhe
thought me too young, whether fhe did not
underftand the advances, or whether fhe would
ferioufly be prudent, fhe had, at thofe times,
a fort of referve which was not unkind, but
which intimidated me without my knowing
the caufe. Though I did not feel for her the
fame real and tender refpect which I felt for
Madam de Warens, I felt more fear and lefs
familiarity. I was perplexed and trembling;
I dared not look at her; I dared not breathe
before her; I neverthelefs dreaded leaving her
more than death. I devoured, with greedy
looks, all I could fee without being perceived;
the flowers of her gown, the end of her pretty
foot, the interval of a white and compact arm
which appeared between her glove and her
ruffle, and that which happened, fometimes,
between the contour of her neck and her
handkerchief. Each object added to the impreffion of others. By dint of looking at what
was to be feen, and even more than was to be

seen, my eyes were confused, my lungs were oppressed, my respiration, every instant more and more impeded, was with trouble kept down, and all I was able to do was to stifle, without noise, the sighs which were very troublesome to me during the silence we often were in. Happily, Madam Basile, employed at her work, did not seem to perceive it. I, however, sometimes saw, by a sort of sympathy, her handkerchief swell frequently enough. This dangerous sight finished my patience, and when I was ready to give way to my transport, she directed a few words to me in an easy voice, which in an instant made me come to myself.

I saw her in this manner several times alone, without there being a word, a motion, or even a look too expressive, which could denote between us the least intelligence. This state, too torturing for me, caused, however, my delight, and I could hardly, in the simplicity of my heart, imagine why I was thus tortured. It seemed these little tête-à-têtes did not displease her neither, at least, she rendered the occasion frequent enough, an attention gratuitous certainly in her, for the use she made of it, or let me make of it.

One day, being tired of the clerk's colloquy, and retiring to her chamber, I hastened to finish my task in the back shop where I was, and followed her. Her chamber-door was half open, I went in without being perceived. She was embroidering near the window, facing that side of the room opposite the door. She could not see me go in, or hear me for the noise of the carts in the street. She was always

ways

ways neatly dreft, that day her attire bordered
on coquettry. Her attitude was graceful, her
head inclining a little forwards, expofed to
view the whitenefs of ner neck; her hair, fet
off with elegance, was decorated with flowers:
there reigned all over her perfon a charm I
had time to examine, but which carried me
beyond myfelf. I threw myfelf on my knees
at the entrance of the room, ftretching my
hands towards her with amorous extacy, quite
certain fhe could not hear me, and not imagining fhe could fee me; but there was a glafs
at the chimney which betrayed me. I don't
know what effect this tranfport had on her;
fhe did not look at me, or fpeak to me, but
turning her fide-face, by a fimple motion of
the finger, fhe fhewed me the mat at her feet.
To leap up, cry out, and fly to the place fhe
pointed to, was all done in the fame inftant;
but it will be hardly believed, I dared under-
take nothing farther, or fay a fingle word, or
raife my eyes towards her, or even touch her
in an attitude fo conftrained, to lean one moment on her knee. I was dumb and immoveable, but not compofed affuredly: every
thing painted in me agitation, joy, gratitude,
and ardent defires uncertain of their object, and
reftrained by the dread of difpleafing, of which
my young heart could not affure itfelf.

She did not appear calmer or lefs timid than
I Uneafy at feeing me there, confounded at
having drawn me there, and beginning to feel
all the confequence of a fign which efcaped
her without reflection, fhe neither encouraged
nor difcouraged me; fhe did not take her eyes

from

from her work; she endeavoured to act as if she did not see me at her feet, but all my stupidity did not prevent me from judging that she partook of my trouble, perhaps of my desires, and that she was withheld by a shame like mine, without its giving me the power of surmounting it. Five or six years older than me, she ought, in my opinion, to take all the freedom herself, and I said to myself, Since she does nothing to excite mine, she does not chuse I should take any. And at this day I believe I thought right; and surely she had too much sense not to see that a novice like me had occasion not only for encouragement, but instruction.

I don't know how this lively and dumb scene would have ended, or how long I might have remained immoveable in this ridiculous and delightful situation, had we not been interrupted.

In the strongest of my agitations I heard the kitchen door open, which joined the chamber we were in, and Madam Basile, alarmed, says to me with hasty voice and gesture, Get up, there is Rosina. In rising in a hurry, I seized her hand, which she held out, I gave it two eager kisses, at the second of which I felt this charming hand press a little against my lips. In my days I never knew so sweet a moment; but the occasion I had lost offered no more, and our young amours stopped there.

This is, perhaps, the reason the image of this amiable woman remains imprinted on the bottom of my heart in so lively colours. It is
heightened

heightened even since I know the world and women. If she had had the least experience, she would have taken another method to animate a young fellow: but altho' her heart was weak, it was honest; she involuntarily yielded to an inclination which hurried her away; 'twas, to all appearance, her first infidelity, and I should have found, perhaps, more to do in vanquishing her modesty than my own. Without going so far, I tasted in her company inexpressible delights. Nothing I ever felt from the possession of women is worth the two minutes I spent at her feet, without even daring to touch her gown. No, there is no enjoyment like that we find in an honest woman we esteem; all is favour with her. A trifling sign of the finger, a hand lightly pressed against my mouth, are the only favours I ever received of Madam Basile; and the remembrance of these favours, so trifling, still transports me when I think of them.

In vain I sought a second tête-à-tête the two following days; it was impossible for me to find an opportunity, and I perceived no inclination in her to favour it. She had even a countenance, not more indifferent, but more reserved than ordinary; and I believe she avoided my looks for fear of not being able sufficiently to govern hers. Her cursed clerk was more mortifying than ever. He became even a banterer and jocose; he told me I should make my way amongst the ladies. I trembled lest I should have been guilty of an indiscretion; and looking upon myself as already familiar with her, I would have made a mystery

     of

of an inclination which till then did not much want it. This made me more circumspect in laying hold of the occasions of satisfying it, and in endeavouring to be certain of some, I found none at all

This is likewise another romantic folly I could never get the better of, and which, added to my natural timidity, has greatly contradicted the clerk's predictions. I loved too sincerely, too perfectly, I dare say it, to be easily happy. Never were passions more lively, and, at the same time, more pure than mine; never was love more tender, more real, and more disinterested. I would have sacrificed a thousand times my happiness to that of the person I loved. Her reputation was dearer to me than life, and never, for all the pleasure of enjoyment, would I have exposed for a moment her peace. This has made me so cautious, so secret, and so careful in my undertakings, that none have ever succeeded. My little success with women was always caused by loving them too much.

To return to the Egistus the fluter: it was most singular, that, in becoming more insupportable, the traitor became more complaisant. From the first minute his lady shewed me kindness, she thought of making me useful in the warehouse. I knew arithmetic pretty well; she proposed his teaching me book-keeping: but the cross fellow received the proposal extremely ill, fearing, perhaps, he might be supplanted. Thus all my work, after engraving, was to copy some accounts and bills, to write over fairly a few books, and translate commercial

cial letters from Italian into French.   All at
once our man took it in his head to return
to the proposal which was made and rejected,
and said he would teach me accompts by
double entry, and make me capable of offering my services to M. Basile on his return.
There was something in his looks, though I
can't tell what, false, artful, and ironical,
which did not inspire confidence.   Madam
Basile, without waiting my answer, to'd him
coldly, I was much obliged to him for his offers,   that she hoped fortune would favour my
deserts, and that it would be a great pity that
one of so much sense should be nothing but a
cle-k

She several times told me she would make
me acquainted with those who could serve
me   She prudently thought it time to send
me from her.   Our dumb declarations happened on Thursday.   On Sunday she gave a
dinner, at which I was present; and likewise
a Dominican friar of a good appearance, to
whom she presented me   The monk treated
me very affectionately, complimented me on
my conversion, and told me several parts of
my history which she had given him the particulars of: then giving me two little strokes on
the cheek with the back of his hand, he told
me to be good, to cheer up, and to go and see
him, in order to talk with more leisure together.   I judged, by the respect every one paid
him, that he was a person of importance, and,
by his paternal tone of voice to Madam Basile,
that he was her confessor.   I recollect also his
decent familiarity was mixed with marks of

esteem

esteem and even respect for his penitent, which at that time made less impression on me than now. Had I had more understanding, how much should I have been touched to have rendered sensible a young woman respected by her confessor.

The table was not large enough for all of us. A side-table was necessary, at which I had the agreeable conversation of the clerk I lost nothing on the side of attention and good eating, several plates were sent to the side-table which certainly were not intended for him. Every thing went well so far, the ladies were very merry, the gentlemen very polite. Madam Basile did the honours of the repast with a charming grace. In the midst of the dinner a chaise was heard to stop at the door, some one comes up; 'tis M. Basile. I see him as if entering this moment, in a scarlet coat with gold buttons; a colour I have since that day detested. M. Basile was a tall, clever man, with an extemely good presence He comes in hastily, and with the air of one who surprises his company, though none were there but his friends. His wife clings around his neck, takes hold of his hands, gives him a thousand caresses, which he receives without returning them. He salutes the company, a plate is brought, he eats. They had scarcely begun talking of his journey, but throwing his eyes on the side-table, he asks, in a severe tone, who that little boy is he sees there? Madam Basile tells him ingenuously. He asks if I lodge in the house? He is told no. Why not? replies he in a rough manner. since he

18

is here in the day-time, he may as well be here at night. The monk took up the conversation, and after a grave and sincere panegyrick on Madam Basile, he made mine in a few words; adding, that, far from blaming the pious charity of his wife, he should be forward in assisting it, since nothing had passed the bounds of discretion. The husband replied in a tone of humour, half of which was stifled, restrained by the presence of the monk, but which was sufficient to let me know he had been informed of me, and that the clerk had served me a trick in his way.

They were scarcely risen from table, but this last, dispatched by his master, came in triumph to signify to me from him, that I must leave the house that instant, and never more set my foot there. He seasoned his commission with every thing which could render it insulting and cruel. I went off without a word, but with a sorrowful heart, not altogether at leaving this amiable woman, but at leaving her a prey to the brutality of her husband. He certainly had a right to take care she was not unfaithful, for although she was prudent, and of good birth, she was an Italian, that is, tender and vindictive; and it was a fault in him, in my opinion, to make use of those means the most likely to bring on the misfortune he dreaded

Such was the success of my first adventure. I endeavoured, by passing and repassing two or three times in the street, to see, at least, her whom my heart grieved for without ceasing: but, instead of her, I saw none but the husband

and

and vigilant clerk, who, on perceiving me, made
a motion with the ell in the shop, more ex-
preſſive than inviting. Finding I was ſo well
watched, I loſt hopes and went no more. I
wiſhed to ſee, however, the patron ſhe had
procured me. Unfortunately I knew not his
name. I rambled ſeveral times, in vain, round
the convent to endeavour to meet him. At
laſt, other adventures baniſhed the charming
remembrance of Madam Baſile; and in a ſhort
time I ſo far forgot her, that, as ſimple and as
much a novice as I was before, I did not remain in danger of pretty women.

Her liberalities had, however, again ſtocked
me a little; very modeſtly nevertheleſs, and
with the precaution of a prudent woman, who
looked on decency rather than dreſs, and who
would prevent me from ſuffering rather than
deck me out. The coat I brought from Geneva was ſtill good and wearable; ſhe added
only a hat and a little linnen. I had no ruffles;
ſhe would give me none, though I greatly deſired them. She thought it ſufficient for me
to be clean; but this was an attention ſhe
need not have recommended while I appeared
before her

A few days after my cataſtrophe, my hoſteſs,
who, as I have ſaid, had ſhewn me friendſhip,
told me ſhe had got me a place, and that a lady
of quality wanted to ſee me. At this word,
I thought myſelf entirely in the road to great
adventures, for that was always uppermoſt in
my thoughts. This was not ſo brilliant as I had
figured it I went to the lady's with the ſervant
who had ſpoke to her of me. She queſtioned
me,

me, examined me; I did not difpleafe her; and immediately entered into her fervice, not abfolutely in quality of a favourite, but in quality of a footman.   I was cloathed in the colour of her people ; the only diftinctio1 was their wearing a fhoulder-knot, and I had none : as there was no lace to the livery, it was nearly a tradefman's coat.   Here was the unexpected term to which, at laft, were pointed all my brilliant hopes.

Madam la Comtefſe de Vercellis, whom I ſerved, was a widow without children, her hufband was a Piedmontefe I always thought her a Savoyard, not being able to perfuade myſelf a Piedmontefe could fpeak fo good French with fo pure an accent.   She was of a middle age, of a noble prefence, a mind well adorned, fond of French literature, and well verfed in it.   She wrote much, and always in French.   Her letters had the expreſſion, and almoft the grace, of Madam de Sevigné's. You might have miftook fome of them for hers. My principal employment, which did not difpleafe me, was to write them from her dictating, a cancer in the breaft, of which fhe greatly fuffered, not permitting her any longer to write herfelf.

Madam de Vercellis had not only much wit, but an elevated and ftrong mind. I attended her laft illnefs. I faw her fuffer and die without once fhewing the leaft weaknefs, without making the leaft effort of conftraint, without quitting her female character, and without imagining any philofophy in all this, a word not then in vogue, and which fhe was not even acquainted

with

with in the fenfe it now bears.   This ftrength
of character was fometimes carried to rudenefs   She always appeared to me to feel as
little for others as for herfelf; and when fhe
did a kindnefs to the unfortunate, it was to do
what was good in itfelf, rather than from true
compaffion.   I experienced a little of this in-
fenfibility during the three months I paffed
with her   It was natural fhe fhould fhew
fome kindnefs to a young perfon of fome views
who was inceffantly under her eye, and think,
finding herfelf dying, that, after her death,
he would want fome affiftance and fupport:
however, whether fhe did not judge me worthy any particular attention, or whether thofe
who furrounded her did not permit her to
think of any but themfelves, fhe did nothing
for me.

I remember, however, very well, her fhewing fome curiofity to know me. She queftioned me fometimes, was glad to fee the letters
I wrote to Madam de Warens, to give an account of my fentiments.   But fhe furely did
not take the right method, by never fhewing
me hers   My heart loved to open itfelf, provided it met with another equally open.   In-
terrogations dry and cold, without any fign
of approbation or blame on my anfwers, gave
me no confidence.   When nothing told me
whether my chatter pleafed or difpleafed, I
was always in fear, and I fought not fo much
to fhew my thoughts as to fay nothing which
could hurt me.   I have fince obferved, that
this dry manner of interrogating people to
know them, is a common trick amongft women
who

who pique themselves on sense. They imagine, that, in not letting their own sentiments appear, they will arrive at penetrating yours the better; but they don't see that they thus take away the resolution of exposing them. A man who is questioned, begins, for that reason only, to put himself on his guard; and if he imagines, that, without thinking of his good, they only want to make him prate, he lies, or conceals, or doubles his attention to say every thing in his own praise, and had rather pass for a fool than be duped in satisfying your curiosity. In fine, it is always a bad method of reading the hearts of others by affecting to hide your own.

Madam de Vercellis never said one word to me that felt of affection, pity, or benevolence. She questioned me coldly. I answered with reserve. My answers were so timid she must have found them mean, and grew tired of them. Towards the last she questioned me no more, and talked of nothing but her service. She judged me less on what I was, than what she had made me; and by dint of seeing me in no other light than that of a footman, she prevented me from appearing any thing else.

I believe I experienced at that time the arch game of underhand interest, which has thwarted me all my life time, and given me a very natural aversion for the apparent order which produces it. Madam de Vercellis having no children, her heir was her nephew, the count of la Roque, who assiduously paid her his court. Besides him, her principal servants, who saw her draw near her end, did not forget

get themſelves; and there were ſo many aſ-
fiduous people about her, it was difficult for
her to think of me. At the head of her affairs was one Lorenzy, an artful fellow, and
whoſe wife, who was ſtill more artful, had ſo
much inſinuated herſelf into the good graces
of her miſtreſs, ſhe was with her rather as a
companion, than a woman who received wages.
She had placed her niece with her as her
chamber-maid; her name was Mademoiſelle
Pontal; a cunning jade, who gave herſelf the
airs of a waiting gentlewoman, and aſſiſted her
aunt in ſo well beſetting their miſtreſs, that ſhe
ſaw but through their eyes, and acted but
through their hands. I had not the happineſs
to pleaſe theſe three perſonages: I obeyed
them, but did not ſerve them; I did not
th nk, that, beſides the ſervice of our common
miſtreſs, I muſt be the valet of her valets. I
was, beſides, a troubleſome perſon to them.
They plainly ſaw I was not in my proper
place. they dreaded their lady might ſee it
likewiſe, and that, if ſhe put me there, it might
decreaſe their portions; for theſe ſort of people, too covetous to be juſt, regard every legacy left to others as taken from their right.
They therefore united to keep me from her
ſight She was fond of writing letters, it was
an amuſement for her in her ſtate; they diſguſted her of it, and got the phyſician to
diſſuade her, pretending it fatigued her. By
pretending I did not know ſervice, they employed in my ſtead two great clowns of chair-
men to be with her. in fine, they managed it
ſo well, that they kept me a week from her
chamber

chamber before she made her will. It is true, I went in afterwards as usual, and was even more assiduous there than any one: for the pains of this poor lady grieved me; the constancy with which she suffered rendered her extremely respectable and dear to me; and I have, in her chamber, shed many sincere tears, without her or any one else having perceived it.

We lost her at last. I saw her expire. Her life had been that of a woman of wit and sense; her death was that of a sage. I can say she rendered the catholic religion amiable to me, by the serenity of soul with which she fulfilled the duties of it, without neglect or affectation. She was naturally serious. Towards her latter end, she took up a sort of chearfulness too equal to be affected, and which was nothing but a counterbalance given by reason itself against the sadness of her situation. She kept her bed the two last days only, and did not cease conversing peaceably with every one. At last, her speech being gone, and already combating the agonies of death, she broke wind loudly. Good, says she, and turned in her bed; she who breaks wind is not dead. These were the last words she pronounced.

She left a year's wages to her under-servants; but, not being set down as one of her family, I had nothing. But the count de la Roque ordered me thirty livres, and gave me the new coat I had on, and which M. Lorenzy would have taken off. He likewise promised to seek me a place, and permitted me to see him I went two or three times to his house, without being able to speak to him. I was easily discouraged,

couraged, I went no more. You will presently see I was to blame.

Why have I not finished all I had to say concerning my abode with Madam de Vercellis! But, though my apparent situation remained the same, I did not come out of her house as I went into it. I carried away from thence the long remembrance of crimes, and the insupportable weight of remorse, with which, though forty years since, my conscience is still loaded, and whose bitter sense, far from growing weaker, grows stronger as I grow older. Who could believe that the faults of a child could have such cruel effects? 'Tis these effects, more than probable, that have caused my heart to get no ease. I have, perhaps, murdered with ignominy and misery an amiable, honest, and estimable girl, who was assuredly much better than I.

The dissolution of a family seldom happens without causing some confusion in the house, and many things to be missed. Such, however, was the fidelity of the servants, and the vigilance of M. and Madam Lorenzy, that nothing was found short of the inventory. Mademoiselle Pontal, only, lost a ribband of a white and rose colour, already much worn. Many better things were within my reach: this ribband only tempted me. I stole it, and, as I did not much hide it, they soon found it on me. They wanted to know whence I got it. I am confused, I hesitate, I stutter, and at last I said, with redness in my face, 'Twas Marion gave it me. Marion was a young Moor, whom Madam de Vercellis had made her cook, when,

ceasing

ceafing to give entertainments, fhe had difcharged her own, having more occafion for
good broths than fine ragouts. Marion was
not only pretty, but had a frefhnefs of colour
to be found only in the mountains, and particularly an air of modefty and mildnefs that
one could not fee without loving; befides,
a good girl, prudent, and of an approved
fidelity. This furprifed them when I named
her. They had almoft as much confidence in
me as in her, and it was judged of importance
to know which of the two was the thief. She
was fent for; the company was numerous, the
count de la Roque was prefent. She comes,
they fhew her the ribband, I accufe her boldly;
fhe remains fpeechlefs and aftonifhed, cafts a
look at me which would have appeafed a devil,
but which my barbarous heart refifts. She
denies, in fine, with affurance, but without
anger, turns towards me, begs me to confider,
not difgrace an innocent girl who never wifhed
me ill; and I, with an infernal impudence,
confirm my declaration, and maintain to her
face that fhe gave me the ribband. The poor
creature began crying, and faid but thefe words,
Ah! Roufleau! I thought you of a good difpofition; you reduce me to mifery, but I would
not be in your place. That's all. She continued
defending herfelf with as much fimplicity as
fteadinefs, but without ufing againft me the
leaft invective. This moderation, compared
to my decifive tone, hurt her. It did not feem
natural to fuppofe on one fide an audaciouf-
nefs fo diabolical, and on the other a mildnefs
fo angelical. They did not feem to determine
entirely,

entirely, but prejudice was for me. In the buftle they were engaged, they did not give themfelves time to found the affair, and the count de la Roque, in fending us both away, contented himfelf with faying, the confcience of the culpable would revenge the innocent. His prediction was not vain; it does not ceafe one day to be fulfilled.

I don't know what became of this victim of my calumny; but there is little appearance of her having been able, after that, eafily to get a good place. She carried with her an imputation cruel to her honour in every manner. The theft was but a trifle, but however it was theft, and, what's worfe, made ufe of to decoy a young fellow: in fine, lies and obftinacy left no hopes of her in whom fo many vices were united. I don't look even on her mifery and being an outcaft as the greateft dangers I expofed her to. Who knows what defpondency and innocence contemned may have led her to   Ah! if the remorfe of having made her unhappy is infupportable, judge how much more cutting it muft be to me for having made her ftill worfe than myfelf.

This cruel remembrance fo much troubles me fometimes, and diforders me to fuch a degree, that I perceive, in my endeavours to fleep, this poor girl coming to upbraid me of my crime, as if it was committed yefterday   Whilft I lived happy, it tormented me lefs; but, in the midft of a life of troubles, it robs me of the fweet confolation of perfecuted innocence. it makes me feel to the quick what I believe I have mentioned in fome of my works, that
re-

remorse sleeps during a prosperous life, but awakens in adversity. I never could determine, however, to disburthen my heart of this load in the breast of a friend. The strictest intimacy never induced me to tell it any one, not even to Madam de Warens. the most I could do was to own I upbraided myself of an atrocious action, but never said in what it consisted. This weight has therefore remained to this day on my conscience without alleviation; and I may say, that the desire of delivering myself from it in some degree, has greatly contributed to the resolution I have taken of writing my Confessions.

I have proceeded openly in that I have just made, and it cannot be thought, certainly, that I have here palliated the heinousness of my crime. But I should not fulfil the object of this book, did I not expose, at the same time, my interior dispositions, and that I dreaded to excuse myself in what is conformable to truth. Never was villainy farther from me than in that cruel hour; and when I accused this unfortunate girl, it is strange, but it is true, my friendship for her was the cause of it. She was present in my thoughts; I excused myself by the first object which offered I accused her of having done what I intended to do, of giving me the ribband, because my intention was to give it her. When I saw her afterwards appear, my heart was racked, but the presence of so many people was stronger than my repentance. I little feared punishment, I dreaded the shame only, but I dreaded it more than death, more than the crime,
more

more than the whole world.   I had been glad to have funk, ftifled in the bofom of the earth: invincible fhame overcame all; fhame only caufed my impudence, and the more I became criminal, the more the terror of acknowledging it rendered me intrepid.   I faw nothing but the horror of being difcovered, publicly de-nounced, myfelf prefent, a robber, liar, and calumniator.   An univerfal perturbation ba-nifhed every other feeling.   Had they let me recover myfelf, I had certainly declared the whole   Had M. de la Roque taken me afide, and faid to me—Don't deftroy the poor girl, if you are guilty, acknowledge it to me—I had inftantly thrown myfelf at his feet; I am perfectly fure of it. But they only intimidated, inftead of encouraging me.   My age is like-wife an allowance it is but juft to make.   I had fcarcely quitted childhood, or, rather, was ftill a child.   In youth enormous crimes are ftill more criminal than in an age of maturity; and weaknefs is much lefs fo, and my fault at bottom was very little more.   For this reafon, its remembrance afflicts me much lefs on ac-count of the mifchief itfelf, than for that which it muft have caufed.   It has even done me this good, of keeping me, for the reft of my life, from every act which tends to-wards committing crimes, by the terrible im-preffion it has left me of the only one I ever was guilty of; and I think I feel my averfion to falfhood grow in a great meafure from the regret of having been able to commit fo black a one.   If it is a crime to be expiated, as I hope it is, all the misfortunes which overwhelm

whelm me in the decline of life muſt have done it, added to forty years of uprightneſs and honour on difficult occaſions; and poor Marion having ſo many avengers in this world, however great my offence was towards her, I have little dread of carrying its guilt with me. This is all I had to ſay on this article. Let me be permitted never to ſpeak of it more.

END OF THE SECOND BOOK.

THE

THE

CONFESSIONS

OF

J. J. ROUSSEAU.

BOOK III.

LEAVING Madam de Vercellis's nearly as I went there, I returned to my old land-lady, and remained there five or six weeks, in which time health, youth, and laziness, often rendered my constitution importunate. I was uneasy, absent, and pensive; cried, sighed, desired a happiness I had no idea of, but whose privation, however, I felt. This situation cannot be described, and few men can even imagine it; because the greatest part have prevented this plenitude of life, at the same time tormenting and delightful, which, in the drunkenness of desire, gives a foretaste of enjoyment. My fired blood incessantly filled my head with girls and women; but not knowing their real use, I possessed them whimsically in idea to my fancy without knowing what more to do with them; and these ideas kept my senses in a disagreeable activity, from which, fortunately, they did not teach me to deliver myself. I had given my life to have

met,

met, for a quarter of an hour, a Miss Goton. But the time was paft when children's play carry them thus far of themfelves. Shame, the companion of a bad confcience, accompanied my years, it had ftrengthened my natural timidity to a degree of rendering it invincible, and never, at that time, or fince, could I arrive at making a lafcivious propofal; unlefs fhe I made it to conftrained me to it, in a manner, by her advances; though certain fhe was not fcrupulous, and almoft fure of being taken at my word.

My ftay with Madam de Vercellis procured me a few acquaintances I kept in with in hopes of making them ufeful. I went to fee, fometimes, among others, a Savoyard abbot, named M Gaime, preceptor to the Count of Mellarede's children. He was a young man little known, but of good fenfe, probity, and underftanding, and one of the honefteft men I ever knew. He was of no ufe as to the object which fent me to him; he had not credit enough to place me. but I received more precious advantages from him, by which my whole life has profited; the leffons of a found morality, and the maxims of a right reafon In the fucceffive order of my inclinations I had always been too high or too low, Achilles or Therfites, fometimes a hero, fometimes a villain. M. Gaime took the pains to put me in my proper place, and to fhew me to myfelf without fparing or difcouraging me. He fpoke to me very honourably of my talents and my genius, but he added, that he faw obftacles arife from them which would prevent me from
                                        making

making the beſt of them, ſo that they would, according to him, ſerve me much leſs in the attainment of fortune, than in reſources to do without it.   He painted me the true picture of human life, of which I had but wrong ideas· he explained to me, how in adverſity a wiſe man may always attain happineſs, and gain that wind which blows him theie; how there is no happineſs without prudence, and how it is that prudence belongs to every condition. He greatly deadened my admiration for gran- deur, in proving to me, that thoſe who lorded it over others were neither wiſer nor happier than they were. He told me one thing, which of- ten occurs to my memory; and that is, if each man could read the hearts of others, there would be more people wiſh to deſcend than aſcend. This reflection, whoſe reality ſtrikes, and has nothing forced, has been very uſeful to me in the courſe of my life, in mak- ing me keep to my lot peaceably.   He gave me the firſt true ideas of honeſty, which my bombaſtic genius had only known to exceſs. He made me underſtand, that the enthuſiaſm for ſublime virtue was of little uſe in ſociety; that in aiming too high you are ſubject to fall, that the continuity of little duties well fulfilled demanded no leſs ſtrength than heroic actions; that you find your account in it much better, both in reſpect to reputation and happineſs; and that the eſteem of mankind was infinitely better than ſometimes their admiration.

To eſtabliſh the duties of a man, you muſt remount to their firſt principles.   Beſides, the ſtep I had taken, whereof my preſent ſituation

was

was the confequence, led us on to talk of religion. It is readily conceived that the honeft M.
Gaime is, at leaft in a great meafure, the
original of the Savoyard vicar. Prudence,
only, obliged him to fpeak with more referve;
he explained himfe'f lefs openly on certain
points, but as to the reft, his maxims, his
fentiments, and his advice, were the fame,
and even the counfelling me to return home,
every thing happened juft as I have given it
fince to the public. Thus, without dwelling
on converfations of which every one may fee
the fubftance, I fhall fay that his leffons, prudent, tho' without an immediate effect, were
as fo many feeds of virtue and religion in my
heart, which were never extinguifhed, and
which waited, to fructify, a more lovely hand.

Though till then my converfion was not
very folid, I was neverthelefs moved. So far
from being tired of his difcourfes, I relifhed
them on account of their clearnefs, their fimplicity, and particularly for a certain intereft of
the heart of which I faw them full. I have an
affectionate turn, and was always endeared to
people lefs in proportion to the good they do
me, than that they wifh to do me, and I am feldom miftaken in them. I, therefore, was very
fond of M. Gaime, I was in a manner his
fecond difciple, and it produced the ineftima-
ble good of turning me from the inclination
to vice my idle life was drawing me into.

One day, thinking of nothing lefs, I was
fent for by the Count de la Roque By continually going, and not feeing him, I grew tired,
and went no more: I thought he had forget
me,

me, or that he had an ill opinion of me. I was miſtaken. He was witneſs, more than once, of the pleaſure I took in fulfilling my duty to his aunt; ſhe even told him of it, and he repeated it to me when I thought little of it. He received me well: told me, that, without amuſing me with empty promiſes, he had ſought to get me a place; that he had ſucceeded; that he would put me in the road of becoming ſomething, and that I muſt do the reſt; that the family he recommended me to was powerful and reſpectable; that I ſhould want no other help to preferment; and that, though treated at firſt as a ſimple ſervant, as before, I might be aſſured, that, ſhould I be judged by my ſentiments and conduct above this ſtate, they were diſpoſed not to leave me in it. The end of this diſcouſe cruelly contradicted the brilliant hopes I had conceived at the beginning of it. What! always a footman? ſaid I to myſelf with a ſpiteful indignation, which confidence ſoon wiped away. I thought myſelf too little made for this place to dread their leaving me there.

He took me to the Count of Gouvon, maſter of the horſe to the queen, and chief of the illuſtrious houſe of Solar. The dignified air of this reſpectable old gentleman rendered the affability of the reception more affecting. He queſtioned me with concern, and I anſwered him with ſincerity. He ſaid to the Count de la Roque, I had an agreeable phyſiognomy which promiſed wit; that it ſeemed to him I had enough, but that was not all, and that he muſt ſee the reſt. Then, turning towards me, Child,

ſaid

said he, the beginnings of almoſt all things are difficult; yours, however, ſhall not be much ſo. Be prudent, and try to pleaſe all here; this is for the preſent your whole buſineſs. As to the reſt, take courage; we'll take care of you. He immediately went to the Marchioneſs of Breil, his daughter-in-law, and preſented me to her, and afterwards to the Abbé de Gouvon, his ſon. This beginning I liked. I had already knowledge enough to know ſo much ceremony was not uſed at the reception of a footman. In fact, I was not treated as one. I dined at the ſteward's table; had no livery; and the Count of Favria, a giddy young man, ordering me behind his coach, his father forbid my going behind any co. ch, or following any body out of the houſe. I waited at table, however, and did in the houſe nearly the ſervice of a footman; but I did it in ſome reſpect with liberty, without being bound particularly to any one. Except a few letters dictated to me, and ſome images I cut for the Count of Favria, I was maſter of almoſt my whole time. This method of acting, which I did not perceive, was ſurely very dangerous; it was altogether very inhuman; for this extremely idle life might have made me contract vices I ſhould not have had without it.

But, luckily, this did not happen. M. Gaime's leſſons had made an impreſſion on my heart, and I ſo much liked them, I ſtole away ſometimes to hear more of them. I fancy thoſe who ſaw me ſteal out, little imagined where I ran to. Nothing could be more ſenſible than the advice he gave me on my conduct. My

be-

beginnings were admirable; I was of an assiduity, an attention, a zeal, which charmed every one. The Abbé Gaime prudently advised me to moderate this first fervour, for fear it should relax, and they should take notice of it. Your beginning, said he, is a rule of what they will expect of you endeavour to spare yourself something to be done hereafter, but take care never to do less than you do now.

As they had examined me but little on my trifling talents, and supposed I had no more than nature had given me, it did not appear, although the Count of Gouvon had promised, that they intended any thing for me. Things happened cross, and I was nearly forgot The Marquis of Breil, son to the Count of Gouvon, was at that time ambassador at Vienna. Some unexpected business happened at court, which was felt in the family, and they were some weeks in an agitation which left little time to think of me. However, till then I had relaxed but little One thing did me good and harm, by keeping me from all external dissipation, I was rendered a little more inattentive to my duty.

Miss de Breil was a young lady about my age, well made, handsome enough, extremely fair. with very black hair, and, though black-eyed, had in her countenance the mild look of a fair woman, which my heart could never resist The court dress, so favourable to young people, shewed her pretty stature, exposed her breast and shoulders, and rendered her complexion still more dazzling from the mourning then worn. You will say, it is not a servant's place

place to perceive thofe things; I was, without
doubt, to blame, but I did perceive them, and
I was not the only one.   The fteward and
valet de chambre talked of them fometimes at
table, with a rudenefs which hurt me greatly.
My head was not, however, fo far loft as to be
quite in love.   I did not forget myelf, I kept
my diftance, and my defires did not even eman-
cipate.   I was happy to fee Mifs de Breil; to
hear her fay any thing which fhewed wit, fenfe,
or modefty.   my ambition, confined to the
pleafure of ferving her, did not go beyond its
bounds   At table I was attentive in making ufe
of them.   If her footman quitted, a moment,
her chair, you faw me placed there that inftant   when not there, I was always oppofite
her, I fought in her looks what fhe wanted;
I watched the moment of changing her plate.
What would not I have given that fhe would
deign to command me, look at me, fpeak to
me but a word!   But no; I had the mortification of being a cypher in her eyes; fhe
did not even know I was there.   However,
her brother, who fometimes fpoke to me at
table, having faid fome words not very obliging, I made him fo fmart and well-turned an
anfwer, fhe remarked it, and threw her eyes
on me.   This look, which was but fhort, did
not fail to tranfport me.   The next day a fecond occafion offered, and I made ufe of it.
There was much company to dinner, when,
to my great furprife, I faw the fteward wait,
his fword by his fide, and his hat on his head.
The converfation by chance turned on the
motto of the houfe of Solar, which was on the

tapeftry in the room with the arms. *Tel fiert qui ne tue pas.* As the Piedmontefe are not in general verfed in the French language, fome of them found in this motto an orthographical error, and faid that in the word *fiert* there fhould be no *t*.

The old Count of Gouvon was going to anfwer, when, looking towards me, he faw I fmiled without daring to fay any thing : he ordered me to fpeak. I then faid, I did not think the *t* too much—that *fiert* was an old French word, which did not derive from the noun *ferus*, fierce, threatening, but from the verb *ferit*, he ftrikes, he wounds—that the motto, therefore, did not appear to me to fay, Many a one threatens, but many a one ftrikes, who does not kill.

The whole company ftared at me, and ftared at each other, without faying a word. Never was fo great a furprife. But what flattered me moft was to fee plainly an air of fatisfaction in the countenance of Mifs de Breil. This difdainful perfon condefcended to caft at me a fecond look, which was at leaft worth the firft; then turning her eyes towards her grandpapa, fhe feemed to expect with a fort of impatience the commendation he owed me, and which he gave me in fact fo full and fo entire, and with an air fo full of fatisfaction, that the whole table was eager to join in chorus. This inftant was fhort, but delicious in every refpect. This was one of thofe uncommon moments which bring back things to their natural order, and revenge merit abafed by the injury of fortune. A few minutes afterwards,

Mifs

Mifs de Breil, raifing her eyes once more on me, begged me, in a voice as timid as it was affable, to bring her fomething to drink. You judge I did not make her wait. But in approaching I was feized with fo great a trembling, that, having filled her glafs too full, I fpilt fome of the water on her plate and even on herfelf. Her brother giddily afked me why I fhook fo? This queftion did not ferve to recover me, and Mifs de Breil reddened like a turkey.

Here finifhed the romance; where you will remark, as with Madam Bafile, and in the whole courfe of my hiftory, that I am not happy in the conclufion of my amours. I in vain attended the antichamber of Madam de Breil, I never more obtained one mark of attention from her daughter. She went out and in without looking at me, and, for my part, I hardly dared look towards her. I was even fo ftupid and fo unfkilled, that one day in paffing fhe let fall her glove; inftead of flying to the glove which I could have covered with kiffes, I dared not ftir from my place, and fuffered it to be taken up by a great lubber of a valet, whom I could have knocked down with pleafure. That I might be entirely intimidated, I had not the good fortune to pleafe Madam de Breil. She not only never ordered my fervice, but never accepted it; and finding me twice in her antichamber, fhe afked me very coldly if I had nothing to do? I was obliged to leave this dear antichamber: at firft I was forry; but other things happening, I foon thought no more of it. I had ample amends

for the disdain of Madam de Breil in the bounty of her father-in law, who at laſt perceived
I was there.   On the evening of the dinner I
ſpoke of, he held a converſation with me half
an hour, with which he ſeemed ſatisfied, and
which highly delighted me.   This good old
gentleman, though a man of ſenſe, had leſs
than Madam de Vercellis, but he was more
compaſſionate, I therefore ſucceeded better
with him.   He told me to attend the Abbé de
Gouvon, his ſon, who was inclined to ſerve
me;   that this inclination, if I would im-
prove it, might be uſeful to me, in helping
me to acquire what I wanted for the deſtina-
tion they intended me.   The next morning I
ran to the Abbé.   He did not receive me as a
ſervant, made me ſit down at the corner of
his fire, and, queſtioning me with the greateſt mildneſs, he found my education, which
had attempted too many things, had completed none.   Seeing particularly I knew a
little Latin, he undertook to teach me more.
It was agreed I ſhould go to him every morning, and I began the next day.   Thus, by
one of thoſe caprices you will often meet in
the courſe of my life, at the ſame time above
and below my condition, I was diſciple and
valet to the ſame family, and in my ſervitude
I had neverthelefs a preceptor whoſe birth
entitled him to be a preceptor to the ſons of
kings only

The Abbé de Gouvon was a younger ſon,
and deſigned by his family to a biſhopric, his
ſtudies, for this reaſon, had been carried farther than is uſual to children of quality. He had
                                                  been

been sent to the university of Sienna, where
he remained several years, and from whence
he brought a pretty strong dose of cruscantism,
in order to be at Turin what formerly the
Abbé de Dangeau was at Paris. A disgust of
theology threw him into the belles-lettres;
this is common enough in Italy to those who
enter the career of prelacy. He had, particularly, read the poets, he wrote Latin and
Italian verse pretty well. He had, in a word,
the necessary taste for forming mine, and giving some choice to the medley with which I
had stuffed my head. But, whether my chatter
had deceived him on my knowledge, whether
he could not support the tediousness of ele-
mentary Latin, he put me too forward; I had
scarcely translated a few fables of Phædrus,
but he threw me into Virgil, where I hardly
understood any thing. It was my fate, as will
be seen in the sequel, often to be taught Latin,
and never to know it. I, nevertheless, laboured zealously enough; and the Abbé la-
vished his attention with a kindness whose remembrance yet moves me. I spent a good
part of the morning with him, as well for my
instruction as for his service, not for that of
his person, for he never suffered me to do any;
but to write under his direction, and to copy.
My function of secretary was much more useful to me than that of pupil. I learnt not
only Italian in its purity, but it gave me a
taste for literature, and some discernment of
good authors, which is not acquired at la
Tribu, and which was afterwards useful to
me, when I worked alone.

G 5

These

These days were those of my life when I could, without romantic projects, most reasonably give into the hope of preferment. The Abbé, well satisfied with me, told every one so; and I was so singularly in his father's favour, the Count of Favria told me he had talked of me to the King. Madam de Breil had likewise left off treating me with that air of contempt. In fine, I became a sort of favourite in the family, to the great jealousy of the rest of the servants, who, seeing me honoured by the instructions of their master's son, felt plainly I was not long to remain their equal.

As much as I could judge of the views they had for me by a few words dropt at random, but on which I did not reflect till afterwards, it appeared to me, the house of Solar, wishing to run the career of embassies, and perhaps open, in time, the road to the ministry, might have been glad to form, before-hand, a person of merit and talents, and who, depending entirely on them, had been able, in time, to have obtained its confidence, and serve it essentially. This project of the Count de Gouvon was noble, judicious, magnanimous, and truly worthy a great, good, and prudent man; but, besides that I did not see its whole extent, it was too judicious for my brain, and required too much constraint. My stupid ambition sought fortune through adventures only; and seeing no woman in all this, this method of preferment seemed slow, painful, and dull; though I ought to have seen it much more honourable and certain, as women had no hand in it: the species of merit they protect,

was

was not, certainly, equal to what was fuppofed in me.

Every thing went on miraculoufly. I had obtained, almoft forced the efteem of every one: the proofs were got through, and I was generally regarded in the family as a young man who had the greateft hopes, who was not in his place, but expected to be there. But my place was not that affigned me by mankind; I was to reach it by a quite different road. I come to one of the characteriftical touches peculiar to me, which it is fufficient to fhew the reader, without adding a reflection.

Although there were many new converts of my fpecies at Turin, I was not fond of, nor ever would fee one of them. But I faw fome Genevefe who were not of them; among others, a M. Muffard, nick-named Wry-chops, a miniature painter, and a diftant relation This M. Muffard found out my abode with the Count de Gouvon, and came to fee me with another Genevefe named Bâcle, whofe companion I, had been during my apprenticefhip. Bâcle was a very amufing, fprightly young fellow, full of jocofe fallies his youth rendered extremely agreeable I am at once infatuated by M. Bâcle, but fo much infatuated as not to be able to quit him. He was foon to depart on his return to Geneva. What a lofs I was going to fuffer! I felt its whole weight. The better, however, to engrofs the whole time he ftayed, I never left him, or rather he never left me; for I was not at firft fo far loft as to go out without leave and fpend the day with him. but very foon, obferving he continually befet me, he

was forbid the house.   I was so much heated,
that, forgetting every thing, except my friend
Bacle, I never went to the Abbé nor the Count,
nor was to be found any longer in the house.
I was reprimanded; but did not listen to it.
They threatened to dismiss me.   This threat
was my ruin; it let me perceive it possible
Bâcle might not go alone.   From that time
I saw no other pleasure, no other fate, no
other happiness than that of making a like
journey; and I saw in it but the ineffable felicity of the journey, at the end of which,
to complete it, I discovered Madam de Warens,
but at an immense distance; for returning to
Geneva I never thought of.   The mountains,
the fields, the woods, the rivulets, the villages,
succeeded each other without end and without
ceasing, with fresh delights.   this heavenly
jaunt seemed to say it would absorb my whole
life.   I recollected with raptures how much
this journey delighted me before.   What
must it be, when, to all the charms of
independence, would be joined that of going
with a companion of my age, of my inclinations,
and of good humour, without restraint, without obligation of going on or resting but
as we pleased?   A man must be a fool, to
sacrifice a like occasion to projects of ambition of a tardy, difficult, and uncertain execution, and which, suppose them realised, were
not worth, in all their splendor, a quarter of
an hour's real pleasure and freedom in youth.

Full of this wise fancy, I conducted myself
so well, I brought about to get myself turned
out, and, to say truth, it was not without
trou-

trouble. One evening, on coming home, the
steward signified to me my dismission by the
Count's order. It was precisely what I wanted; for seeing, in spite of myself, the extra-
vagance of my conduct, I added, to excuse it,
injustice and ingratitude, thus imagining to
throw the blame on others, and be justified in
my own eyes in an act of necessity. I was
told from the Count Favria to speak to him the
next morning before my departure; but as
they perceived my brain was turned, and that
I was capable of not observing it, the steward
put off till after this visit the present intended
me, and which assuredly I had badly earned;
for, not having left me in the state of a valet, I
had no fixed wages.

The Count of Favria, young and giddy as
he was, shewed on this occasion the most reasonable language, and, I almost dare advance,
the tenderest, so much did he recal, in the most
flattering and touching manner, the attention of
his uncle and the intention of his grandfather.
In fine, having brought, in lively colours, to
my view, what I sacrificed to my ruin, he offered to make my peace, exacting, as the only
condition, that I no more saw the sorry wretch
who had seduced me.

It was so plain he did not say this of himself, that, in spite of my stupid inconsiderate-
ness, I felt all the bounty of my old master,
and it touched me but this dear journey was
so imprinted on my imagination, that nothing
could balance its charms I was absolutely
beyond my wits, I grew flouter, more har-
dened, affected haughtiness, and arrogantly
an-

answered, that, as they had given me my dismiffion, I had taken it; that it was too late to retract; and that, whatever might happen to me, I was refolved never to be turned twice out of the fame houfe. At this, the young man was juftly irritated, gave me the epithets I deferved, turned me out of his room by the fhoulders, and fhut the door on my heels. For my part, I went off triumphantly, as one who had gained the greateft victory; and, for fear of having a fecond combat to fuftain, I had the bafenefs to depart without going to thank the Abbé for his kindnefs.

To conceive how far I carried my delirium at this time, you fhould be acquainted to what a point my mind is fubject to be heated by the leaft trifle, and with what force it plunges into the idea of an object which attracts it, however vain this object might fometimes be. The moft foolifh, the moft childifh, the moft unaccountable plans, footh my favourite idea, and fhew me fuch a probability as to give into them. Would one believe, that, at near nineteen, I fhould build my hopes on an empty phial for the fubfiftence of the reft of my days? Well, hearken.

The Abbé de Gouvon made me a prefent, a few weeks before, of an Hern fountain, very pretty, which delighted me. By continually playing this fountain, and talking of our journey, we imagined, the wife Bâcle and I, that one might affift the other, and prolong it. What in the world could be fo curious as an Hern fountain? This principle was the foundation on which we built our fortune.

We

We were to assemble the country-people of each village around our fountain, and there meals and good living were to fall on us in greater abundance, as we were both persuaded provisions cost those who gather them nothing, and that when they did not stuff strangers with them, 'twas mere ill-nature. We imagined every where feastings and rejoicings, supposing that, without any other expence than the wind of our lungs, and the water of our fountain, we should be defrayed in Piedmont, in Savoy, in France, and all over the world. We laid out endless projects for our journey, and directed our course northward, rather for the pleasure of crossing the Alps, than for the supposed necessity of stopping at last any where.

This was the plan on which I began the campaign, abandoning, without regret, my protector, my preceptor, my studies, my hopes, and the expectation of an almost certain fortune, to begin the life of an absolute vagabond. Farewel the capital, farewel the court, ambition, vanity, love, the fair, and all the brilliant fortune whose hopes had guided me the preceding year! I set off with my fountain and my friend Bàcle, a purse scantily garnished, but an heart leaping with joy, and thinking of nothing farther than this strolling felicity to which I had at once confined my shining projects.

I made this extravagant journey almost as agreeably, however, as I expected, but not exactly in the same manner; for, although our fountain amused, a few minutes, in the public-houses, the landlord and his waiters,

ers, we muft, neverthelefs, pay at parting. But that troubled us little: we thought to make ufe heartily of this refource when our money failed only An accident faved us the trouble; the fountain broke near Bramant, and it was quite time; for we felt, without daring to fay fo, that it began to tire us This misfortune rendered us gayer than before, and we laughed heartily at our inconfideratenefs in having forgot that our cloaths and fhoes were wearing, or imagining we could replace them by the diverfion of our fountain. We continued our journey as merrily as we began it, but drawing a little nearer an end, where our exhaufted purfes made it neceffary to arrive.

At Chambery I became penfive, not on the folly I had committed; never did man fo foon or fo well make up his mind on the paft; but on the reception which awaited me at Madam de Warens's, for I looked on her houfe exactly as my paternal one. I wrote to her on my entrance at the Count de Gouvon's; fhe knew the footing I was on, and in complimenting me fhe gave me fome wife leffons on the manner in which I ought to anfwer the kindnefs they fhewed me. She looked on my fortune as certain, did I not deftroy it by my own fault. Wh t would fhe fay on feeing me? It never once came into my head that fhe might fhut her door againft me, but I dreaded the vexation I fhould caufe her, I dreaded h r reproaches, fharper to me than want. I refolved to endure all in filence, and do every thing to appeafe her. I faw in the

uni-

univerfe but her alone; to live out of her favour could not be.

I was moft uneafy about the companion of
my journey; which I was forry to tell him,
and whom I dreaded I fhould not be able eafily
to get rid of. I prepared this feparation by
living cooly with him the laft day: the droll
fellow comprehended me; he was more crazy
than fottifh. I imagined this change would
affect him; I was wrong; my friend Bàcle
was not to be affected. We had hardly fet our
foot in Annecy, but he fays to me, Thou art at
home, fhook me by the hand, bid me farewel,
turned on his heel, and went off. I never heard
of him fince. Our acquaintance and our friendfhip lafted together about fix weeks; but the
effects have lafted as long as myfelf.

How did my heart beat in approaching the
houfe of Madam de Warens! My legs trembled under me, my fight was overcaft, I faw
nothing, heard nothing, nor fhould have known
any one; I was forced to ftop feveral times to
breathe and recover my fenfes. Was it the
fear of not obtaining the aid I wanted that
troubled me to this degree? At the age I was
of, does the dread of ftarving produce thofe al-
larms? No, no, I fpeak it with as much
truth as pride, never at any time of my life
could intereft or indigence boaft of having re-
joiced or oppreffed my heart. In the courfe
of a life unequal and memorable by its viciffi-
fitudes, often without an afylum or bread, I
always faw with the fame eye both opulence
and mifery. At a pinch I had begged or ftole
like another, but feel no uneafinefs at being reduced

duced to it. Few men have fuffered like me, few have fhed fo many tears in their lifetime; but never did poverty, or the dread of falling into it, caufe me to heave a figh or drop a tear. My foul, proof againft fortune, acknowledged no true happinefs or real mifery but thofe which did not depend on her, and it was when nothing was wanting on the fide of neceffaries I felt myfelf the unhappieft of mortals.

I had fcarcely appeared before Madam de Warens but her countenance cheared me. I leaped at the firft found of her voice, I ran to her feet, and in the tranfports of melting joy I preffed my lips to her hand. For her part, I don't know whether fhe had heard of my affair, but I faw little furprife in her countenance, and not the leaft uneafinefs. Poor little fellow! fays fhe, in a foothing tone, you are here again then. I knew very well you were too young for this journey; I am very glad, however, it did not turn out fo bad as I dreaded. She afterwards made me tell my whole ftory, which was not long, and told very faithfully, concealing, however, a few articles, but without fparing or excufing myfelf.

The queftion was my lodging. She confulted her maid. I dared not breathe during this deliberation; but when I heard I was to fleep in the houfe, 'twas with trouble I contained myfelf; and I faw my little bundle carried to the room intended for me, nearly as St. Preux faw his chair carried back to Madam de Wolmar's. I had, to complete it, the

the pleafure of learning that this favour was not to be tranfient, and, at a time they thought me attentive to other things, I heard her fay, They may talk as they will, but fince Providence has brought me him again, I am determined not to abandon him.

Here I am then, at laft, fixed at her houfe. 'Tis not, however, from hence I date the happy part of my life, but it ferved to prepare it. Although this fenfibility of heart, which makes us really enjoy each other, is the work of nature, and perhaps a production of organization, it calls for a fituation to unfold itfelf. Without thefe occafional caufes, a man born with fine feelings would feel nothing, and go out of the world without having known his exiftence. Such, nearly, had I been till then, and fuch had I perhaps always been, had I never known Madam de Warens, or if, having known her, I had not lived long enough with her to contract the gentle ufe of the affectionate fentiments fhe infpired me with. I dare advance, he who feels only love, does not feel the greateft charms of this life. I am acquainted with another feeling, lefs impetuous perhaps, but more delightful a thoufand times, which fometimes goes with love, and is fometimes feparated from it. This fentiment is not friendfhip alone neither; it is more luxurious, and tenderer: I don't imagine it can act for one of the fame fex; at leaft, I know friendfhip if ever man knew it, and never felt it for any one of my friends. This is not clear, but it will be in what follows; feelings are not to be thoroughly defcribed but by their effects.

She

She lived in an old houfe, but large enough to have a room of referve, in which fhe received compiny, and in which fhe lodged me. This room was in the paffage where I have faid we had our firft conference, and beyond the little brook and gardens you perceived the country This fight was to the young inhabitant not an indifferent thing. It was, fince Boffey, the firft verdure I had feen before my window. Always enclofed by walls, I had never before my eyes but the tiles or the ftreet. How charming and fweet was this novelty ! It very much increafed my difpofition to tendernefs. I looked on this pleafing landfcape as one of the favours of my dear protectrefs : it feemed fhe placed it there on purpofe for me, I placed myfelf peaceably there by her fide ; I faw her every where between the flowers and the verdure ; her charms and thofe of the fpring were blended in my eyes My heart, till then compreffed, found itfelf more expanded in this fpace, and my fighs were breathed with more freedom among thefe orchards.

The magnificence I had feen at Turin was not found at Madam de Warens's, but I found cleanlinefs, decency, and a patriarchal abundance that oftentation never reaches. She had very little plate, no china, no game in her kitchen, or foreign wine in her cellar ; but both were well furnifhed, at every one's fervice, and in her earthen cups fhe offered excellent coffee. Whoever came there was invited to dine with her or at her houfe, and never workman, meffenger, or traveller, went away without eating or drinking. Her houfe-hold

hold was compofed of her own maid from Fribourg, pretty enough, named Merceret, a valet from her own country, named Claude Anet, whom we fhall fpeak of afterwards, a cook, and two hackney porters for her vifits, which happened rarely. This is a great deal for two thoufand livres a year; her little income, if well managed, would have, neverthelefs, fufficed to all this, in a country where the land is extremely good, and money very fcarce. Unhappily, œconomy was never her favourite virtue, fhe ran in debt, fhe paid; money ferved as a wedge, and fo it went on.

The manner her houfe was conducted was precifely what I would have chofen; you may think I took the advantage of it with pleafure. I was leaft pleafed with fitting fo long at table. She with trouble fupported the firft fmell of foup or meat. This fmell almoft made her faint, and her difguft lafted fome time. She came to by degrees. chattered, but did not eat. 'Twas half an hour before fhe tried the firft bit. I had dined three times in this time; my meal was finifhed long before fhe began hers. I kept her company, and thus eat for two without finding myfelf worfe for it. In fine, I gave into the agreeable fentiment of the well-being I found with her, fo much the readier, as this well-being I enjoyed was mixed with no uneafinefs on the means of fupporting it. Not being yet in the ftrict confidence of her affairs, I fuppofed her in a ftate of always continuing the fame I found the fame pleafure in her houfe afterwards, but, better informed, of her real fituation, and feeing
fhe

she anticipated on her income, I did not enjoy it with the same tranquillity. Foresight has always, with me, spoiled enjoyment. I saw futurity in vain ; I never could avoid it.

From the first day the easiest familiarity was entertained between us to the same degree it continued during the rest of her life. Little Dear was my name, Mamma hers ; and we always lived together, Little Dear and Mamma, even when years had almost effaced the difference between us. I find that these two names marvellously render the idea of our tones, the simplicity of our manners, and particularly the relation of our hearts. She was to me the tenderest of mothers, who never sought her pleasure, but always my good ; and if sense formed a part in my passion for her, 'twas not to change its nature, but only to render it more exquisite to infatuate me with the charm of having a mamma young and pretty, whom it delighted me to caress : I say to caress, in a literal sense ; for she never thought of sparing her kisses or the tenderest maternal caresses, and it never entered my heart to abuse it. You will say we had, however, at last, relations of another sort : agreed ; but stay a little ; I can't say all at once.

The sight of her, at our first interview, was the only instant truly passionate she ever caused me ; and even that instant was the work of surprise. My indiscreet looks were never busied under her handkerchief, though a plumpness little covered in this part might very well have drawn them there. I had neither transports nor desires with her ; I was in
a ra-

a ravishing calm, enjoying without knowing what. I could thus have spent my life and eternity without being tired an instant. She was the only person with whom I never found a dryness of conversation, which is the greatest of punishments, from the obligation of supporting it. Our tête-à-têtes were not so much discourse as an inexhaustible prattle, which to put an end to must be interrupted. So far from the obligation of talking, I was rather obliged to impose myself that of forbearing. By long contemplating her projects, she lost herself in thought. Well, I let her remain so; I said nothing, I gazed on her, and was the happiest of men. I had, besides, another singular trick. Without pretending to the favours of privacy, I continually fought it, and enjoyed it with a passion which degenerated to fury, if it was interrupted. As soon as any one came in, man or woman, 'twas equal to me, I went out murmuring, not being able to remain a third in her company. I went and counted the minutes in her antichamber, cursing, a thousand times, these eternal visitors; nor could I conceive how they had so much to say, because I had still more.

I never felt my whole passion for her, but when I did not see her. When I saw her I was contented only; but my uneasiness at her absence carried me to a degree of grief. The necessity of living with her gave me transports so melting as often to draw tears. I shall never forget one great holiday, whilst she was at vespers, I took a walk out of town, my mind filled

filled with her image and an ardent defire to
fpend my days with her. I had fenfe enough
to fee, that, at prefent, it was not poffible, and
that a happinefs I fo well relifhed would be
fhort. This gave my contemplation a forrow-
fulnefs which had, however, nothing gloomy
in it, and which was allayed by flattering hope.
The found of the bells, which always fingu-
larly affected me, the finging of birds, the
clearnefs of the weather, the fweetnefs of the
landfcape, the houfes fcattered and rural, in
which I placed in idea our common abode, all
this ftruck me with an impreffion fo lively, fo
tender, fo penfive, and fo touching, that I faw
myfelf, as in extacy, tranfported to thofe happy
times, and in thofe happy abodes, where my heart,
poffeffing every felicity that could delight it,
tafted them in raptures inexpreffible, without
ever thinking of fenfual voluptuoufnefs I never
remember to have launched into futurity fo
forcibly, and with fuch illufions, as at that
time ; and what ftruck me moft in the recollection of this conceit, when it was realized,
was to find the objects exactly fuch as I had
imagined them. If ever the dream of a man
awake had the air of a prophetic vifion, it was
certainly this I was deceived in its imaginary
duration only ; for the days, and the years, and
the whole life, paffed in an unalterable tranquillity, but in effect it all lafted but an inftant. Alas ! my moft certain happinefs was
but a dream. Its accomplifhment was almoft
-inftantly followed by fleeping no more.
  I fhould never end, was I to enter into
the particulars of all the follies the remem-
                                        brance

brance of this dear Mamma caufed me to act, when I was not in her fight. How many times I have kiffed her bed, in thinking she had lain there; my curtains, all the furniture of the room, in thinking they were hers, that her dear hand had touched them; even the floor on which I laid myfelf, thinking she had walked there. Sometimes, even in her prefence, the greateft extravagancies have fallen from me, that only the moft violent paffion feemed able to infpire. One day at table, at the time of her putting a bit in her mouth, I cry out I fee a hair in it; she fpits it out on her plate, I greedily lay hold of and fwallow it. In a word, between me and the moft paffionate lover there was but only one effential difference, and that renders my ftate almoft inconceivable to reafon.

I was returned from Italy, not altogether as I went, but as, perhaps, never at my age any one came back. I brought back from thence, not my virginity, but my maidenhead. I had felt the progrefs of years, my troublefome conftitution, at laft, declared itfelf, and its firft eruption, extremely involuntary, gave me apprehenfions for my health, which paint, better than any thing elfe, the innocence in which I had lived till that time. But my fears being foon removed, I learnt this dangerous fupplement which diverts the courfe of nature, and faves young people of my humour many diforders at the expence of their health, their vigour, and fometimes their life. This vice, which shame and timidity find fo convenient, has, befides, great enticements for live-

ly imaginations; that is, to difpofe, in a manner, at will, of the whole fex, and to make
the beauties which tempt them ferve their
pleafures without the neceffity of obtaining
their confent. Seduced by this fatal advantage,
I laboured to deftroy the found conftitution
nature had given me, and to which I had given
time to form ftrongly.   Add to this difpofition
the locality of my prefent fituation; lodged at
a pretty woman's, careffing her image in my
heart, feeing her inceffantly in the day-time,
at night furrounded by objects which recal
her to my mind, fleeping in the bed I know
fhe has flept in.   What ftimulants! Whatever
reader reprefents them to himfelf, looks on
me as already half dead.   Quite the contrary:
that which fhould have deftroyed me, precifely faved me, at leaft for fome time.   Drown-
ed in the pleafure of her company, the ardent
defire of paffing my days in it, abfent or prefent, I always faw in her a tender mother, a
beloved fifter, a delightful friend, and nothing
farther.   I always faw her fo, continually the
fame, and faw nothing but her.   Her image,
always prefent, left room for no other; fhe
was, to me, the only woman exifting; and
the extreme gentlenefs of fentiment with which
fhe infpired me, not allowing my fenfes time
to awaken for others, defended me from her
and the whole fex   In a word, I was moderate becaufe I loved her.   From thefe effects,
which I badly relate, tell me who can, of
what fpecies was my paffion for her? For my
part, all I can fay of it is, that, if this feems
very extraordinary, what follows will appear
much more fo.   I fpent

I spent my time the most agreeably, employed on things which pleased me least. These were either plans to adjust, bills to write out, receipts to transcribe : there were herbs to pick, drugs to pound, stills to watch: and in the midst of all this came crowds of travellers, beggars, visits of all sorts. You must entertain, all at once, a soldier, an apothecary, a prebendary, a lady of fashion, and a layic. I inveighed, I grumbled, I swore, I wished all this cursed medley at the devil. For her who took every thing gaily, my fury made her laugh till tears came down her cheeks ; and that which made her laugh still more was, to see me grow the more furious, as I could not help laughing myself. These little intervals, which gave me the pleasure of growling, were delightful; and if a chance guest came in during the dispute, she knew how to make the most of it for amusement, in maliciously prolonging the visit, and casting now and then a glance at me, when I could willingly have beat her. She could hardly abstain from bursting, on seeing me, constrained and moderate from decency, give her the looks of a demon, whilst, from my heart, even in spite of me, I thought it all exceeding pleasant.

All these things, without pleasing me in themselves, nevertheless, amused me, because they made a part of a manner of being which charmed me. Nothing that was done around me, nothing they made me do, was after my taste, but every thing was after my heart. I believe I should have arrived at a fondness for

H 2   medicine,

medicine, had not my difgust to it produced
toying fcenes which inceffantly diverted us:
it was, perhaps, the firft time this art produced a like effect. I pretended to know by
the fmell a pound of drugs, and it is pleafant
to think I was feldom miftaken. She forced
me to tafte the moft deteftable drugs. 'Twas
in vain I ran off, or would have contended;
in fpite of my refiftance and my horrible
grimaces, in fpite of myfelf, and my teeth,
when I faw thofe lovely fingers approach my
mouth, I muft open it and fuck. When all
her little apparatus was affembled in one room,
to hear us run and halloo amidft the burftings
of laughter, you would have thought we were
acting a farce, inftead of making opiate or
elixir.

My time was not, however, fpent entirely
in this foolery. I had found a few books in
the room I flept in · the Spectator, Puffendorf,
St. Evremond, the Henriade. Though I did not
preferve my old paffion for reading, yet, to
fill my leifure, I read a little of all thefe The
Spectator, particularly, pleafed me much, and
was ufeful to me. The Abbé de Gouvon had
taught me to read lefs eagerly, and with more
reflection, I edified more by ftudy. I accuftomed myfelf to reflect on elocution, and on
elegant conftruction; I exercifed myfelf in
difcerning pure French from the country dia-
lect. For inftance, I was corrected in an orthographical fault I made with all our Genevefe, by thefe two verfes of the Henriade,

Soit un ancien refpect pour le fang de leurs maîtres
Parlut encor pour Lui dans le cœur de ces traîtres

The

The word *parlât*, which struck me, taught me that there must be a *t* in the third person of the subjunctive; instead of which I wrote and pronounced *parla*, as in the present of the indicative.

Sometimes I chattered with Mamma on my study; sometimes read to her, I took great pleasure in it, I exercised myself in reading well, and it was useful to me. I have said she had a well-cultivated understanding. It was then in all its prime. Several men of letters had endeavoured to render themselves agreeable to her, and had taught her to judge of works of merit. She had, if I am allowed to say it, a taste a little Proteftant, she talked of none but Bayle, and extolled St. Evremond, who had been long dead in France. But that did not prevent her from knowing good literature, and conversing very well on it. She had been brought up in choice society, and coming to Savoy still young, she had loft, in the pleasing company of the nobility of the country, the affected tone of the country of Vaud, where the ladies take wit for sense, and cannot speak but in epigrams.

Though she had seen the court but little, she threw a rapid glance around it, which was, to her, sufficient to know it. She always kept friends there, and, in spite of secret jealousy, in spite of the murmurs her conduct and debts excited, she never loft her pension. She had a knowledge of the world, and the spirit of reflection, which knows to draw advantages from that knowledge. It was the favourite subject of her conversations, and precisely, considering my chimerical notions,

H 3 the

the fort of inſtruction I moſt wanted.   We
read together la Bruyere : he pleaſed her more
than Rochefaucault, a dull and mortifying
book, principally for youth who do not love to
ſee man as he is.   When ſhe moralized, ſhe
ſometimes loſt herſelf a little by wandering;
but, with a kiſs now and then of the lips or
hands, I kept my patience, and her tedıouſ-
neſs was not tıreſome.

This life was too pleaſing to laſt.   I ſaw it,
and the uneaſineſs of ſeeing it terminate was
the only thing which diſturbed its enjoyment.
With all our foolery, Mamma ſtudıed me, obſerved me, queſtioned me, and built up for
my fortune vaſt projects which I could very
well have done without.   Happily, it was net
ſufficient to be acquainted with my inclinations, my taſte, and my trifling talents ; occaſions were to be ſought to make them uſeful,
and theſe were not the buſineſs of a day.
Even the prejudices the poor thing had conceived in favour of my merit, retarded the
time of employing it, by making her more
difficult on the choice of the means. in fine,
all went as I could wiſh, thanks to the good
opinion ſhe had of me ; but ıt was to be low-
ered, and then farewel eaſe ! One of her relations, named M. d'Aubonne, came to ſee
hei.   He was a man of great underſtanding,
cunning, and a genius for projects like herſelf, but did not ruin himſelf by them, a ſort
of adventurer   He came from offering the
Cardinal of Fleury the plan of a lottery, extremely well compoſed, but which was not
reliſhed.   He was going to offer it the court
of

of Turin, where it was adopted and put in execution.   He stayed some time at Annecy, and became enamoured with the housekeeper, who was a very amiable person, very much of my taste, and the only one I saw with pleasure at Mamma's.   M. d'Aubonne saw me, his kinswoman talked to him about me; he undertook to examine me, to see what I was proper for, and, if he found any genius in me, endeavour to place me.

Madam de Warens sent me to him two or three mornings following, on pretext of an errand, and without acquainting me with any thing of it before-hand He took an excellent method of making me chatter, spoke freely with me, put me under as little restraint as possible, talked to me of trifles and on all sorts of subjects; all without seeming to observe me, without the least affectation, and as if, pleased with me, he would converse without restraint. I was delighted with him.   The result of his observations was, that, whatever my exterior and my animated physiognomy might promise, I was, if not absolutely a fool, at least a boy of very little sense, without ideas, almost without acquirements, in a word, a very shallow fellow in all respects, and that the honour of becoming some day the parson of a village was the greatest fortune I ought to aspire to.   Such was the account he gave of me to Madam de Warens. This was the second or third time I was thus judged, it was not the last, and the decree of M Masseron has been often confirmed.

The cause of these judgments is too much connected with my character not to want an

explanation : for, in confcience, it is plainly
feen I cannot fincerely fubfcribe to them , and
that, with all poffible impartiality, whatever
Meffieurs Mafferon, d'Aubonne, and many
others have faid, I cannot take their word for
them.

Two things, almoft inalliable, unite in me,
without my being able to conceive the manner. A conftitution extremely violent, impetuous and lively paffions, and ideas flowly
produced, confufed, and which never offer
till after the proper time   You would think
my heart and mind do not belong to the fame
individual. Sentiment quicker than light fills
my foul, but, inftead of enlightening, it fires
and dazzles me.   I feel every thing and fee
nothing.   I am tranfported, but ftupid ; I
muft be cool to think.   What aftonifhes is,
that I have my feeling pretty fure, penetration,
and even delicate wit, provided they'll wait
for me . I can make an excellent impromptu
at leifure, but in an inftant I never wrote or
faid any thing clever.   I could hold a pretty
converfation by the poft, as the Spaniards, it is
faid, play at chefs   When I read that ftroke of
the Duke of Savoy's, who turned round, keeping on his journey, to cry out, *At your throat,
Paris merchant !* I faid, I am here.

This flownefs of thought, joined to the vivacity of feeling, is not in my converfation
only; I have it when alone alfo, and when I
write.   My ideas are difpofed in my head with
the greateft difficulty . they circulate dully;
they ferment till they move me, heat me, give
me palpitations; and, amidft all this emotion,
I fee

I see nothing clearly ; I cannot write a single word ; I must wait. Insensibly this vast emotion is suppressed, the chaos is dispersed ; each thing takes its place, but slowly, and after a long and confused agitation. Have you ever seen an opera in Italy ? In changing the scenes there reigns a disagreeable disorder on these grand theatres, which lasts a considerable time : the decorations are all intermixed ; you see in every part a pulling and hauling about which gives pain ; you think the whole is turning topsy-turvy. By degrees, every thing is, however, brought to its place, nothing is wanting, and you are greatly surprised to find a ravishing sight succeed this long tumult. This piece of work nearly resembles that which operates in my brain, when I would write. Had I first known how to wait, and then render, with all their beauties, the things thus painted there, few authors would have surpassed me.

Thence comes the extreme difficulty I find in writing. My manuscripts scratched out, blotted, mixed, not legible, attest the trouble they cost me. Not one but I was obliged to transcribe four or five times before it went to the press. I never could do any thing, the pen in hand, opposite a table and paper . 'twas in my walks, amidst rocks and woods , 'twas in the night, during my slumbers ; I wrote in my brain, you may judge how slowly, particularly to a man deprived of verbal memory, and who, in his life, never could retain six verses by heart. Some of my periods have been turned and winded five or six nights in

my

my head before they were in a state for going on paper. From thence, likewise, I succeed better in works which demand labour, than in those which must have a certain airiness; as letters, a style I could never get the tone of, and whose occupation is to me the greatest of punishments. I write no letters on the most trifling subject, which do not cost me hours of fatigue; or, if I would write immediately what strikes me, I can neither begin nor end; my letter is a long and confused verbosity; with trouble I am understood when it is read.

I am not only troubled to render my ideas, but even in receiving them. I have studied mankind, and think myself a tolerable good observator: nevertheless, I cannot see any thing in that I perceive; I see clearly that only I recollect, and I have no knowledge but in my recollections. Of all that's said, of all that's done, of all that passes in my presence, I know nothing, I penetrate nothing. The external sign is all that strikes me. But afterwards the whole returns again; I call to mind the time, place, tone, look, gesture, circumstance; nothing escapes me. Then, from what they said or did, I find out what they thought, and it is very seldom I mistake.

So little master of my judgment alone by myself, judge what I must be in conversation, when, to speak a-propos, you must think at one and the same time of a thousand things. The sole idea of so many conformities, of which I am sure to forget at least some one, suffices

to

to intimidate me.   I don't even comprehend
how they dare talk in company : for at each
word you muſt paſs in review before every
perſon there; you muſt be acquainted with
every man's character, know their hiſtory, to
be aſſured of ſaying nothing which might of-
fend ſome of them ; in which thoſe who frequent the world have a great advantage : knowing better on what to be ſilent, they are ſurer
of what they ſay; and with all that, they often
let fall abſurdities.   Judge, therefore, of him
who falls there from the clouds ! It is almoſt
impoſſible he ſhould talk a minute with impunity.   In private converſations there is another inconvenience I think worſe ; the neceſſity of always talking.   When you are ſpoke
to, you muſt anſwer ; and if nothing is ſaid,
you muſt revive the converſation.   This inſupportable conſtraint only would have diſguſted me of ſociety.   I find no toture like
that of the obligation of ſpeaking inſtantly and
continually.   I don't know whether this proceeds from my mortal averſion to all ſubjection;
but it is ſufficient that if I muſt abſolutely talk,
I infallibly talk nonſenſe.   What ſtill is more
fatal, inſtead of knowing when to be ſilent, if
I have nothing to ſay, 'tis then, the ſooner to
pay my debt, I have the fienzy of wanting to
talk   I haſten to ſtammer quickly words
without ideas, very happy when they mean
nothing at all.   Striving to hide my folly, I
ſeldom fail to ſhew it.

I believe here is enough to make it underſtood, how, without being a fool, I have

never-

neverthelefs often paffed for one, even with people who were thought good judges; fo much the more unhappily, as my phyfiognomy and eyes promifed more, and that this expectation fruftrated, renders to others my ftupidity more fhocking. This detail, which a peculiar occafion gave birth to, is not unneceffary to what follows. It contains the key to many extraordinary things I have been obferved to do, which is attributed to a favage humour I have not. I fhould love fociety like another, was I not certain of appearing there, not only to difadvantage, but quite different to what I am. My determination to write and hide myfelf from the world is precifely that which fuited me. Myfelf prefent, my parts had never been known, or even fufpected; and this happened to Madam Dupin, though a woman of fenfe, and though I lived in her houfe feveral years. She has often told me fo herfelf fince that time. However, all this fuffers certain exceptions, and I fhall come over it again in the courfe of the work.

The meafure of my talents thus fixed, the ftate I was fit for thus defigned, there was no farther queftion, for the fecond time, but the fulfilling my vocation. The difficulty was my not having gone through my ftudies, or knowing Latin enough even to become a prieft. Madam de Warens propofed fending me to be inftructed fome time at the Seminary. She mentioned it to the Superior, he was a Lazarift, named M. Gros, a good-natured, half-blind, meagre, grey-haired little

tle man, the moſt ſpiritual and the leaſt pedantic Lazariſt I have known; which, in fact, is
not ſaying much.

He ſometimes came to Mamma's, who welcomed him, and ſometimes let him lace her ſtays;
an employment he willingly undertook. Whilſt
he was thus in office, ſhe ran from one ſide of
the room to the other, doing ſometimes one
thing, ſometimes another. Drawn by the lace,
the Superior followed grumbling, nnd ſaying
every minute, Well, Madam, hold ſtill then.
It produced a ſcene funny enough.

M. Gros heartily gave into Mamma's project. He was contented with a moderate ſalary, and undertook my inſtruction. Nothing
was wanting but the Biſhop's conſent, who
not only conſented to it, but would pay it
himſelf. He likewiſe permitted me to remain
in the ſecular habit, till they could judge by
a trial of the ſucceſs they might hope.

What a change! I muſt ſubmit. I went to
the Seminary as to the place of execution.
What a doleful place is a ſeminary; eſpecially
to him that comes from the houſe of a pretty
woman! I carried one book only, which I
begged Mamma to lend me, and which was
a great reſource to me. You would not gueſs
what ſort of a book this was; a muſic book.
Among the talents ſhe cultivated, muſic was
not forgot. She had voice, ſung paſſably, and
played the harpſichord a little. She had had the
complaiſance to give me a few leſſons of muſic,
and ſhe was obliged to bring me from far, for
I hardly knew the muſic of our pſalms. I had,
nevertheleſs, ſo great a paſſion for this art, I
want-

wanted to make a trial of exercifing myfelf alone. The book I carried with me was not of the eafieft neither; 'twas Clerambault's cantatas.   My application and obftinacy may be conceived, when I tell you, that, without knowing either tranfpofition or quantity, I arrived at decyphering and finging the firft ricitative and the firft air of the cantata of Alpheus and Arethufa : it is true, this air is fcanned fo juft, you need only recite the verfes with their meafure to catch the air.

There was a curfed Lazarift at the Seminary who undertook me, and made me deteft the Latin he would have taught me. He had fhort, thick, black hair, a gingerbread face, a bull's voice, the looks of a pole-cat, a wild boar's briftles inftead of a beard ; his fmile was from ear to ear; his limbs played like pullies in a puppet-fhow : I have forgot his odious name ; but his frightful, precife figure I have retained; it is with trouble I recollect him without horror.   I think I fee him yet in the paffage, pulling forward with grace his old fquare bonnet as a fign to come into his room, more dreadful to me than a cell. Judge of the contraft between fuch a mafter for the difciple of a Court Abbé.

Had I remained two months at the mercy of this monfter, I am perfuaded my head would not have refifted. But the good-natured M. Gros, who perceived I was dull, eat nothing, and grew thin, guelfed the caufe of my uneafinefs, it was not difficult. He took me from the clutches of the animal, and by a ftill more ftriking contraft put me to the mildeft
of

of men. He was a young Abbé from Faucigne-
ran, named M. Gâtier, who studied at the
Seminary, and, from complaisance for M. Gros,
and I believe from humanity, was so kind as
to take from his own studies that time he gave
to the direction of mine. I never saw a physiognomy more touching than M. Gâtier's.
He was fair, with a beard inclining to carroty.
He had the common appearance of people of his
province, who under a heavy outside hide a
deal of good sense, but that which truly cha-
racterised him was a sensible, kind, and affable
heart. He had in his large blue eyes a mixture
of good temper, tenderness, and sadness, which
engaged one to wish him well. In the looks,
in the tone of this poor young man, you
would have said he foresaw his destiny, and
that he felt himself born to misfortune.

His character did not contradict his physiognomy. Made up of patience and complaisance, he seemed to study with me rather than
instruct me. Less would have done to have
gained my esteem; his predecessor had rendered that extremely easy. Nevertheless, though
he bestowed so much time on me, and though
each of us did all in his power, and although
he took an exceeding good method, I advanced
little with much labour. It is singular, that,
with conception enough, I could never learn
any thing by masters, except my father and
M. Lambercier. The little I have got since I
learnt alone, as you will see. My reason, dis-
claiming every kind of yoke, cannot submit
to the laws of the moment. Even the dread of
not learning prevents my attention. For fear

of

of tiring him who fpeaks, I feign to underftand him ; he goes on, and I underftand nothing of it.   My reafon will march at its own
hour ; it cannot fubmit to another's.

The time of ordination being arrived, M.
Gâtier returned to his province a deacon. He
carried with him my grief, my attachment, and
my gratitude. I fent up prayers for him, which
were no more heard than thofe I made for myfelf.   A few years afterwards I heard, that,
being curate of a parifh, he had a child by a
girl, the only one, though he had an extremely tender heart, he had ever known.   This
was a dreadful fcandal in a diocefe fo feverely
governed.   Priefts, according to what is right,
muft get none but married women with child.
Becaufe he failed in this law of conveniency,
he was fent to prifon, defamed, and turned
out. I don't know whether afterwards he was
able to fettle his affairs ; but the fenfe of his
misfortunes, deeply graven on my mind, returned when I wrote Emilius, and, uniting
M. Gâtier with M. Gaime, I made of thefe
two worthy priefts the original of the Vicar of
Savoy.   I flatter myfelf the imitation did not
difgrace its models.

Whilft I was at the Seminary, M d'Aubonne
was obliged to leave Annecy.   M*** took it
in his head to be angry that he made love to his
wife   'Twas imitating the gardener's dog;
for though Madam *** was amiable, he lived
on poor terms with her, and treated her fo
brutally a feparation was talked of.   M***
was an ugly fellow, black as a mole, knavifh
as an owl, and who by dint of oppreffions
                                          ended

ended by being himself driven out. It is said the Provincials revenge themselves on their enemies by songs ; M. d'Aubonne revenged himself on his by a comedy : he sent this piece to Madam de Warens, who shewed it me. It pleased me, and inspired me with a fancy to write one, to try whether I was in effect that blockhead the author had pronounced me ; but it was not till I came to Chambery I executed this project, in writing The Lover of Himself. Thus when I said, in the preface to this work, I wrote it at eighteen, I curtailed a few years.

'Twas about this time an adventure refers to, of little importance in itself, but which in respect to me has had effects that have made a noise in the world when I had forgot it. I had, every week, permission to go out. I have no occasion to mention the use I made of it. One Sunday, being at Mamma's, a fire broke out in the buildings of the Cordeliers, joining the house she occupied. This building, in which was their oven, was stuffed full of dry faggots. The whole was in a short time on fire. The house was in great danger, covered by the flames the wind brought there. They began to remove in haste, and carry the goods into the garden, which was opposite my former windows, and beyond the brook I have already spoken of. I was so affrighted, I threw indifferently out at the window every thing I laid hold of, even a large stone mortar, which at any other time I could hardly have lifted : I was going to throw, equally, a large looking-glass, if some one had not held me.

The

The good Bishop, who that day came to see Mamma, did not remain idle neither. He took her to the garden, where he began prayers with her and all those who were there; so that, coming up some time afterwards, I saw every one on their knees, and I fell on mine. During the holy man's prayer, the wind changed, but so suddenly and so a-propos, that the flames, which covered the house, and had already entered the windows, were driven to the other side of the court, and the house received no damage. Two years afterwards, M. de Bernex being dead, the Antonines, his old brethren, began to collect the pieces which might serve towards his beatification. At the instance of Father Boudet, I joined to these pieces an attestation of the fact I have just stated, in which I did well; but in that I did ill was giving this fact as a miracle. I had seen the bishop at prayers, and during his prayers I saw the wind change, and even extremely a-propos. this I might have said and certified; but that one of these two things was the cause of the other, I ought not to have attested, because I could not know it. However, as far as I can recollect my ideas at that time, a sincere catholic I was in earnest. The fondness for miracles so natural to the human heart, my veneration for this virtuous prelate, the secret pride of having myself contributed to the miracle, aided in seducing me; and if this miracle had been the effect of the most ardent prayers, it is certain I might have attributed to myself a part of it.

More

More than thirty years afterwards, when I published the Letters from the Mountain, M. Freron diſcovered this certificate, I don't know by what means, and made uſe of it in his paper. I muſt own the diſcovery was fortunate, and the patneſs appeared even to me extremely pleaſant.

I was fated to be the outcaſt of all conditions. Although M. Gâtier gave the leaſt unfavourable account poſſible, they ſaw it was not proporiioned to my labour, which had nothing encouraging to carry my ſtudies farther. The Biſhop and the Superior, therefore, gave me over, and I was returnéd to Madam de Warens as a perſon not worth the making even a prieſt of; in other reſpects a good lad, ſay they, and not vicious: this cauſed her, in ſpite of every diſpiriting prejudice againſt me, not to abandon me.

I brought back to her, in triumph, the muſic-book I had made ſo good uſe of. My air of Alpheus and Arethuſa was nearly all I had learnt at the Seminary. My remarkable taſte to this art gave riſe to a thought of making me a muſician. The occaſion was convenient. She had muſic at leaſt once a week at her houſe, and the muſic-maſter of the cathedral, who directed this little concert, came very often to ſee her. He was a Pariſian, named M. la Maître, a good compoſer, very lively, very gay, ſtill young, pretty well made, little ſenſe, but on the whole a very good kind of man. Mamma made me acquainted with him; I was all to him, and did not diſpleaſe him: the ſalary was mentioned; 'twas agreed on.

In

In fhort, I went to him, paffed the winter there the more agreeably as the houfe was not more than twenty paces from Mamma's; we were with her in a moment, and fupped there very often together.

You may judge, the life of the band, always finging and gay with the muficians and the finging-boys of the choir, pleafed me more than the Seminary and the fathers of St. Lazarus. However, this life, though more free, was not lefs even and regular. I was made to love independence, and never abufe it. During an intire fix months, I never went out once, but to Mamma's or church; nor did I even wifh it. This interval is one of thofe in which I lived in the greateft calm, and that I recolleĉt with the greateft pleafure. In the divers fituations I have found myfelf, fome of them have been marked with a fentiment of well-doing, that, in bringing them again to my memory, I am as affeĉted by them as if I was ftill there. I not only recal time, place, and perfons, but every encompaffing objeĉt, the temperature of the air, its fmell, its colour, a certain local impreffion which is not felt but there, and whofe lively remembrance carries me there again. For inftance, all they repeated at the band, all they fung at the choir, all they did there, the charming and noble drefs of the canons, the priefts chafubles, the chanters mitres, the mufician's perfons, an old lame carpenter who played the counter-bafs, a little fpark of an abbé who played the violin, the tattered caffock which, after laying down his fword, M. le Maitre put over his fecular coat,

coat, and the beautiful fine surplice with which he covered the tatters to go to the choir; the loftiness with which I went, *holding my little flute, placing myself at the orcheftra in the gallery*, for a little end of a recitative M. le Maitre had composed on purpose for me; the good eating that awaited us afterwards, the good appetite we carried there, this concourse of objects, brought back in a lively manner, has an hundred times charmed me by my memory, as much or more than in reality. I have always retained a feeling inclination for a certain air of *Conditor alme sfyderum*, which goes by iambics; because, one Sunday in Advent, I heard from my bed this hymn sung before day, on the steps of the cathedral, according to a custom of this church. Mifs Merceret, Mamma's woman, knew a little of music. I shall never forget the little anthem *Afferte* which M. le Maitre obliged me to sing with her, and which his miftrefs heard with so much pleafure. In fine, all down to the good-natured girl Perrine, who was so good a girl, and whom the singing-boys teazed to madnefs, every thing of the remembrance of those times of happinefs and innocence often returns to enrapture and afflict me.

I lived at Annecy almoft a twelvemonth without the leaft reproach; every one was fatisfied with me. Since my return from Turin I had committed no follies, nor did I commit any whilft I was with Mamma. She always conducted me properly; my attachment to her was become my sole paffion, and a proof it was not a foolish paffion, my

heart

heart formed my reaſon.   It is true, this only
ſentiment, abſorbing, in a manner, all my facul-
ties, put it out of my power to learn any thing,
not even muſic, though I made every effort.
But it was not my fault; none could be more
willing; aſſiduity was not wanting. I was inattentive and penſive; I ſighed; what could I
do?   Nothing was wanting to my progreſs
which depended on me; but that I might commit freſh follies, a ſubject only was neceſſary.
This ſubject preſented itſelf; chance ſettled
all, and, as you will afterwards ſee, my fool-
iſh head made uſe of it.

One evening, in the month of February, in
very cold weather, as we were all around the
fire, we heard a knocking at the ſtreet door.
Perrine takes the lanthorn, goes down, and
opens. a young man comes in with her, comes
up ſtairs, introduces himſelf with an eaſy air,
and pays M. le Maitre a ſhort and well-turned
compliment ; ſays he is a French muſician,
that the bad ſtate of his purſe obliged him to
act the vicar, to get on his road.   At this
word of French muſician, M. le Maitre's
good-natured heart leaped for joy; he was
paſſionately fond of his country and his art.
He receives the young traveller, offers a lodging he ſeemed much to want and accepted
without much ceremony.   I obſerved him,
whilſt he warmed himſelf and chattered, till
ſupper time Short of ſtature, but very ſquare,
he had I don't know what ill in his make,
without any particular deformity; he was,
one may ſay, hump-backed with flat ſhoulders, but I believe he limped a little. He had

on a black coat rather worn than old, which
was falling to pieces, a very fine but very
dirty shirt, beautiful fringed ruffles, spatter-
dashes into each of which he might have put
both his legs, and, to keep the snow from
him, a little hat to carry under his arm. In
this odd equipage he had, nevertheless, something noble which his conversation did not
contradict; his look was delicate and agreeable; he talked with ease and well, but not
very modestly. Every thing shewed him a
young libertine, who had education, and did
not go begging as a beggar, but as a fool. He
told us his name was Venture de Villeneuve,
that he came from Paris, that he lost his way,
and, forgetting a little his story of musician,
he added he was going to Grenoble, to see
a relation who was of the parliament.

During supper music was talked of, and he
talked well. He knew all the greatest virtuosi,
every actor, every actress, every pretty woman, every nobleman. He seemed perfectly
acquainted with all that was said, but a subject was scarcely begun, but he threw into
the conversation some joke which made them
laugh and forget all they had said. This
was on Saturday; the next day we had music
at the cathedral. M. le Maitre asked him to
sing there, *With all my heart*, asks him his
part? *The counter-tenor*, and talks of something else. Before going to church they offer
him his part to peruse; he did not look at it.
This gasconade surprised le Maitre: he whis-
pers to me and says, You'll see he does not
know a single note in music. I am much afraid
of

of it, ſay I. I follow them extremely uneaſy. When they began my heart beat with terrible force; for I was very much inclined to wiſh him ſucceſs.

I had ſoon reaſon to recover myſelf. He chanted his two recitatives with all the juſtice and taſte imaginable, and what more is, with an extremely pretty voice. I was hardly ever more agreeably ſurpriſed. After maſs, M. Venture was complimented to the ſkies, by the canons and muſicians, to which he replied joking, but always with a deal of grace. M. le Maitre embraced him heartily; I did the ſame: he ſaw I was very glad, and it ſeemed to give him pleaſure.

You will agree, I am ſure, that, after being infatuated by M. Bâcle, who, take him together, was but a booby, I might be infatuated of M. Venture, who had education, talents, wit, and the knowledge of the world, and who might paſs as a pleaſing libertine. 'Twas what happened to me, and what might have happened, I believe, to any other young man in my place, ſo much the more readily too, if he had a better knack of perceiving merit, and a better reliſh to be engaged by it: for Venture had merit beyond contradiction, and he had a very rare one at his age, that of not being forward in ſhewing his acquirements. It is true, he boaſted of many things he knew nothing of, but of thoſe he knew, which were pretty numerous, he ſaid nothing. he waited the occaſion of ſhewing them, he made uſe of them without forwardneſs, and this had the greateſt effect. As he ſtopped
at

at each thing without speaking of the rest, you could not tell when he would finish. Sportful, waggish, inexhaustible, ensnaring in his conversation, always smiling, never laughing, he said in a most elegant tone of voice the rudest things, and made them pass. Even the modestest women were astonished why they suffered him. It was in vain they knew they should be angry, they had not the power He desired none but prostitutes ; I don't believe he was made for fortunes, but he was made for rendering infinitely agreeable the society of those who had them.   It was unlikely, that, with so many agreeable talents, in a country where they are well understood and cherished, he long remained within the sphere of a musician.

My inclination to M. Venture, more reasonable in its cause, was likewise less extravagant in its effects, though more active and more durable, than that I had towards M. Bacle. I loved to see him, hear him ; all he did seemed charming, all he said seemed oracles : but my infatuation did not extend so far as not to be separated from him I had in the neighbourhood a good preservative against this excess Besides, finding his maxims very good for him, I saw they were not for me to make use of : I wanted another kind of pleasure, of which he had no idea, and of which I dared not speak to him, certain he would have ridiculed me.   However, I wanted to ally this attachment to that which governed me. I spoke of it with transport to Mamma ; le Maitre spoke to her of it with commendation. She confented to his introduction ; but the interview did not fucceed at all he thought her formal, fhe faw him a libertine ; and being alarmed at my making fo bad an acquaintance, fhe not only forbid my bringing him there again, but fo ftrongly pointed out to me the danger of this young man, I became a little more circumfpect towards him, and, very happily for my morals and my brains, we were foon feparated.   M. le Maitre had the taftes of his art : he loved wine : at table, however, he was fober, but at work in his clofet he muft drink.   His maid knew it fo well, that, as foon as he prepared his paper for compofing, and had taken his violoncello, his pot and glafs arrived an inftant afterwards, and the pot was replenifhed from time to time.   Without ever being abfolutely drunk, he was almoft always fuddled , and faith it was pity, for he was a perfon effentially good, and fo merry, Mamma called him no other than *Little Cat*   Unfortunately, he was fond of his talent, worked much, and drank the fame.   This reached his health, and at laft his humour, he was fometimes fufpicious, and eafily offended. Incapable of rudenefs, incapable of difrefpect to any one, he never fpoke an ill word, even to his finging-boys   But neither would he be treated difrefpectfully; that was but juft. The evil lay in his having little knowledge ; he did not diftinguifh tone or character, and often took the huff at nothing.

The ancient chapter of Geneva, where, formerly fo many princes and bifhops thought it an honour to fit, has loft, in their exile, its ancient fplendor, but has preferved its loftinefs. To be admitted, you muft be either a gentleman or a doctor of Sorbonne. If there is a pardonable pride after that derived from perfonal merit, it is that merit birth gives. Befides, all priefts, who have laity in their pay, treat them, in general, haughtily enough. 'Twas thus the canons often treated poor le Maitre. The chanter, particularly, named M. Abbé de Vidonne, who in other refpects was a very accomplifhed man, but too full of his nobleffe, had not always that refpect for him his talents merited; the other could not well put up with his difdain. In the Paffion-week of this year they had a fharper difpute than ufual at a dinner of inftitution the Bifhop invited the canons to, and where le Maitre was always afked. The chanter did him fome injuftice, and faid fomething harfh, which the other could not digeft. He that moment took a refolution of leaving them the following night, and nothing could make him defift from it, though Madam de Warens, whom he went to take leave of, did all in her power to appeafe him. He could not renounce the pleafure of being revenged on his tyrants, in leaving them diftreffed in the Eafter holidays, a time when they were in the greateft want of him. But that which diftreffed him likewife, was his mufic he would take with him, this was not eafy. It formed a cheft pretty large and very heavy, not to be taken under one's arm.

Mamma did as I had done, and would yet do, in her place. After many efforts to retain him,

him,

him, feeing him refolved to go at all events, fhe determined to help him as much as depended on her. I dare advance fhe owed it him. Le Maitre had devoted himfelf, in a manner, to her fervice. Whether in what belonged to his art, or what depended on attention, he was entirely at her commands; and the heart, which went with it, gave his complaifance an additional value. She therefore did no more than return a friend, on an effential occafion, what he had done for her, in detail, during three or four years; but fhe had a foul, which, to fulfil fuch duties, had no occafion to be told it was for her. She fent for me, ordered me to follow M. le Maitre at leaft as far as Lyons, and to remain with him as long as he wanted me. She has told me fince, that the defire of removing me from Venture had a great fhare in this bufinefs. She confulted Claude Anet, her faithful fervant, as to the conveyance of the cheft. His advice was, that inftead of taking a pack-horfe, which would infallibly difcover us, we muft, at dark, carry the cheft on our fhoulders to a certain diftance, and then hire an afs in fome village, to carry it to Seyffel, when, being in the French territories, we had nothing more to fear. This counfel was followed we departed at feven the fame evening, and Mamma, on pretext of paying my expences, fwelled the petty purfe of the poor Little Cat by an addition which was not ufelefs. Claude Anet, the gardener, and I, carried the cheft as we could to the neareft village, where an afs relieved us, and the fame night we reached Seyffel.

I think

I think I have obferved fomewhere, that there are inftants in which I fo little refemble myfelf, I might be taken for another man of a quite oppofite character.   You are going to fee an example of this   M. Reydelet, vicar of Seyffel, was canon of St Peter's, of courfe M. le Maitre's acquaintance, and one of thofe he fhould hide himfelf moft from.   My advice was, on the contrary, to go and introduce ourfelves there, afk him to lodge us on fome pretext, as coming by confent of the chapter. Le Maitre relifhed this notion, which rendered his vengeance mocking and pleafant.   We therefore went boldly to M. Revdelet's, who received us well.   Le Maitre told him he was going to Bellay, by defire of the Bifhop, to direct his mufic in the Eafter holidays; that he fhould return in a few days. and, in fupport of this lie, I ftuffed in an hundred more, fo natural, that M. Reydelet thought me a fmart lad, and fhewed me kindnefs with a thoufand careffes   We were well treated, well lodged; M Reydelet did not know how to make enough of us, and we feparated the beft friends in the world, promifing to ftay longer on our return.   We could hardly ftay till we were alone to burft with laughing, and I declare it takes me again now on thinking of it; for you could not imagine a trick better fupported or more happy.   It had made us merry the whole journey, had not M. le Maitre, who inceffantly drank, and reeled about, been attacked two or three times by a fit, to which he became very fubject, very much refembling an epilepfy.   This threw us into a diforder that

I 3   af-

affrighted me, and which I thought to extricate myself from as I could.

We went to Bellay to pass the Easter holidays, as we had told M. Reydelet; and though we were not expected, we were received by the music-master, and welcomed by every one, with the greatest pleasure. M. le Maitre was esteemed for his skill, and merited it. The music master at Bellay honoured him with his best compositions, and endeavoured to obtain the approbation of so good a judge; for, besides being a connoisseur, le Maitre was equitable, not at all jealous, no flattering parasi e. He was so superior to all those provincial music-masters, and they so well knew it, they regarded him less as a brother artist than as their head.

Having passed, very agreeably, four or five days at Bellay, we left it, and continued our journey, without any other accident than those just mentioned. Arrived at Lyons, we were lodged at Notre Dame de Pitié; and while waiting for the chest, that, favoured by another falsity, we had embarked on the Rhone, by the care of our good protector, M Reydelet, M le Maitre went to see his acquaintances, among others Father Caton, a Cordelier, of whom we shall speak afterwards, and the Abbé Dortan, Count of Lyons. Both received him well, but betrayed him, as you will presently see, his good fortune ended at M Reydelet's.

Two days after our arrival at Lyons, as we were passing up a little street, not far from our inn, le Maitre was taken with one of his fits;

fits, this was fo violent, I was feized with terror. I cried out, called help, named his inn, and begged he might be carried there; then, whilft they affembled and crowded around a man fallen without fenfe and foaming in the middle of the ftreet, the only friend on which he depended, left him I took the inftant when no one thought of me, turned the corner of the ftreet, and difappeared —Thanks to Heaven, I have finifhed the third painful declaration! Did many more remain, I fhould abandon the work I have begun.

Of all I have hitherto faid, a few veftiges are to be found in the places I have lived; but that I mean to fpeak of in the following book is entirely unknown. They are the greateft extravangancies of my life, and it was lucky they did not finifh worfe. But my head, raifed to the tone of a foreign inftrument, got out of its diapafon, it came back of itfelf; I then quitted my follies, or at leaft I committed thofe which better agreed with my natural difpofition. This period of my youth is that I have the moft confufed idea of. Nothing paffed at this time which fufficiently engaged my heart to trace in a lively manner its remembrance; and it will be ftrange, if, in fo many turnings and windings, in fo many fucceffive changes, I do not tranfpofe time or place. I write abfolutely from memory, without notes, without matter, which might remind me of it. There are events of my life as prefent as when they happened; but there are gaps and voids I cannot fill up but by the affiftance of recitals as confufed as their

re-

remaining remembrance. I may, therefore, have erred, and may err again on trifles, until the time I had more certain marks to conduct me; but in that which is of real import to the subject, I am sure of being exact and faithful, as I shall always endeavour to be on every thing· this may be depended on.

As soon as I had quitted M le Maitre, my resolution was taken, and I set out on my return to Annecy. The cause and the mystery of our departure had given me great concern for the safety of our retreat; and this concern, wholly employing me, had caused a diversion for some days from that which called me back again: but the moment security had produced tranquillity, the governing sentiment took place again. Nothing flattered me, nothing tempted me; I had no other desire than that of returning to Mamma. The tenderness and reality of my affection for her, had rooted from my heart all imaginary projects, all the follies of ambition. I saw no other happiness than that of living with her, nor did I take one step without feeling I was removing from this happiness. I therefore returned there as fast as possible. My return was so quick, and my mind so distracted, that, although I recollect with so much pleasure all my other journeys, I have not the least remembrance of this. I recollect nothing at all of it, except my departure from Lyons, and my arrival at Annecy. Judge if this last period could ever quit my memory at my arrival, I found Madam de Warens was no more there; she was gone to Paris.

I ne-

I never rightly knew the secret of this journey. She would have told me, I am very certain, had I preſſed her; but never was man leſs curious of knowing the ſecrets of friends. My mind ſolely employed on the preſent, it fills up its whole extent, its whole ſpace, and, except paſt pleaſures, which are henceforth my enjoyments, there is not the leaſt ſpare corner for that which exiſts no more. All I thought I perceived in the little ſhe ſaid to me of it was, that, by the revolution cauſed at Turin in the abdication of the King of Sardinia, ſhe dreaded being forgot, and wanted, favoured by the intrigues of M. d'Aubonne, to get the ſame ſupport of the Court of France, which, ſhe has often told me, ſhe would have preferred; becauſe the multiplicity of great intereſts prevents one's being ſo diſagreeably watched. If it was ſo, it is ſurprifing, that, on her return, they did not receive her with more indifference, and that ſhe always enjoyed her penſion without interruption. Many people thought her charged with ſome ſecret commiſſion, either from the Biſhop, who at that time had ſome affairs at the Court of France, where he himſelf was obliged to go, or from ſome one ſtill more powerful, who knew to prepare for her a happy return. It is certain, if that was ſo, the Ambaſſadreſs was not badly choſen, and that, ſtill young and beautiful, ſhe had every neceſſary talent for ſucceeding in a negotiation.

END OF THE THIRD BOOK.

THE
CONFESSIONS
OF
J. J. ROUSSEAU.

BOOK IV.

I ARRIVE and don't find her there. Judge of my surprise and my affliction! 'Twas then the regret of having shamefully abandoned M. le Maitre began to pinch. It was still sharper when I learnt the accident that had happened to him. His chest of music, which contained his whole fortune, this choice chest, saved with so much trouble, had been seized on coming into Lyons by the vigilance of the Count Dortan, to whom the Chapter had wrote to apprize him of this private theft. Le Maitre claimed, in vain, his property, his livelihood, the labour of his whole life. The property of this chest was certainly subject to dispute; there was none. The affair was decided in the very instant by the laws of the strongest, and poor le Maitre thus lost the fruit of his talents, the labours of his youth, and the dependence of his old-age.

Nothing was wanting to the shock I received to render it overwhelming. But I was of an age

when

when great grief has little power, and soon forged myself consolation. I expected to hear very soon from Madam de Warens, though I did not know her direction, and she was ignorant of my return; and as to my desertion, every thing reckoned, I did not think it so culpable. I had been useful to M. le Maitre in his retreat; 'twas the only service I could do. Had I remained with him in France, I could not have cured his disorder, I could not have saved his chest, I should only have doubled his expences, without being able to serve him in the least. Thus it was I then saw the affair; I now see it otherwise. It is not when a dirty action is just committed, it torments us, it is on the recollection of it long afterwards; for its remembrance does not die.

The only means of hearing from Mamma was to wait; for how was I to seek for her at Paris, and with what make the journey? There was no place so certain as Annecy to know sooner or later where she was. I therefore remained there. But I conducted myself bad enough. I did not go to see the Bishop who had patronized me, and might still have patronized me. My protector was no more with me, and I dreaded a reprimand on our evasion. I went still less to the Seminary. M. Gros was gone. I saw none of my friends: I should have went with pleasure to see the Intendant's lady, but dared not. I did worse than all that. I found out M. Venture again, of whom, though so much delighted with him, I had not thought since my departure. I found him again shining and welcomed in

I 6   every

every part of Annecy, the ladies tearing him from each other. This fuccefs quite turned my head. I faw nothing but M. Venture, and he almoft made me forget Madam de Warens. The better to benefit by his leffons, I propofed lodging with him; he confented. He lodged at a fhoemaker's; a droll, pleafant fellow, who in his gibberifh called his wife nothing but flut; a name fhe much deferved. He had wranglings with her, which Venture took'care to promote, in feeming to wifh the contrary. He had the ftrangeft dry fayings, which in his country accent had the fineft effect; 'twas fcenes which would make one burft with laughing. Thus paffed the mornings without thought. At two or three we eat a bit of fomething. Venture went out into companies, where he fupped; and I went a walking alone, meditating on his great merit, admiring and coveting his rare talents, and curfing my ugly ftars, that had not called me to this happy life. Ah! how little I knew of it! Mine had been an hundred times more charming, had I been lefs a fool, and known better how to enjoy it.

Madam de Warens had taken with her Anet only; fhe had left Merceret, her chamber-maid, of whom I have already fpoken. I found her ftill occupying her miftrefs's apartment Mifs Merceret was a little older than myfelf, not pretty, but agreeable enough; a good-natured girl from Fribourg, without malice, and in whom I knew no other fault than muttering a little at her miftrefs. I went to fee her pretty often; fhe was an old acquaintance, whofe fight called to my mind one more dear, and

made

made me love her. She had several acquaintances; among others, a Miss Giraud, of Geneva, who, for my sins, took it in her head
to have an inclination for me. She continually
begged Merceret to bring me to her house;
I consented to go, because I loved Merceret
well enough, and that we found other young
people there I saw with pleasure. As for Miss
Giraud, who did nothing but ogle me, nothing can be added to the aversion I had for
her. When she came near me with her hard
black snout besmeared with Spanish snuff, I
could hardly abstain from heaving. But I
took patience, and, except that, I was well
enough pleased with these girls; whether to
court Miss Giraud, or myself, each strove to
surpass the other in feasting me. I saw nothing but friendship in all this. I have since
thought it my own fault I did not see more;
but then I did not think so.

Besides, mantua-makers, chambermaids, little tradeswomen, did not tempt me much. I
wanted young ladies. Every one to his fancy,
that was always mine, nor do I think with
Horace on that point. It is not, however, at
all, the vanity of rank which attracts me, 'tis
a complexion better preserved, prettier hands,
a more graceful attire, an air of delicacy and
neatness over all their person, more taste in
the manner of their dress and their expression,
a gown finer and better made, a leg and foot
more delicately formed, ribbands, lace, hair
better disposed. I should always prefer less
beauty, having more of all this. I myself find
this

this preference very ridiculous; but my heart gives into it in fpite of me.

Well, this advantage offered too, and it depended on me only to lay hold of it. How I love to fall from time to time on the agreeable minutes of my youth! They were fo fweet, fo fhort, fo rare, and I tafted them at fo cheap a rate! Ah! their remembrance only brings back to my heart pure delights I greatly ftand in need of to revive my fpirits, and fupport the forrows of my remaining years.

Aurora one morning appeared fo beautiful, that, dreffing myfelf precipitately, I hafted into the country to fee the rifing fun. I relifhed this pleafure with all its charms; 'twas the week after Midfummer-day. The earth in its gayeft cloathing was covered with herbs and flowers; the nightingales, whofe warbling grew near its end, feemed to outvie each other in raifing their lovely notes; the whole of the feathered race, biding in chorus farewel to fpring, welcomed the birth of a fine fummer's day, of one of thofe heavenly days which are not feen at my age, and which the penfive foil I now inhabit never faw.

I infenfibly left the city, the heat increafed, and I walked under the fhade in a valley by the fide of a brook. I hear behind me the fteps of horfes, and the voice of fome girls, who feemed in trouble, but who did not laugh lefs heartily. I turn round, they call me by my name; I approach, and fee two young people of my acquaintance, Mifs de G*** and Mifs Galley,

ley, who, not being the beſt of horſewomen, knew not how to get their horſes acroſs the brook   Miſs de G*** was a young lady from Berne, very amiable, who, for ſome folly of her age, having been ſent out of her country, had imitated Madam de Warens, where I had ſometimes ſeen her; but not, like her, getting a penſion, ſhe was very happy in her acquaintance with Miſs Galley, who, having contracted a friendſhip for her, engaged her mother to let her have her as a compa-nion, until ſomething could be done with her. Miſs Galley, one year younger than her, was prettier; ſhe had ſomething of I don't know what more delicate and ſmart about her, ſhe was likewiſe at the ſame time ſlender and well ſhaped, which is for a girl a happy thing. They were tenderly fond of each other, and the kind character of the one and the other muſt long entertain this harmony, if no lover came to diſturb it.   They told me they were going to Toune, an old caſtle belonging to Madam Galley; they begged my aſſiſtance in making their horſes go on, not being able to do it themſelves : I would have whipped their horſes, but they feared my being kicked, and their being thrown.   I had recourſe to another expedient : I took the bridle of Miſs Galley's horſe, and pulling him after me, I croſſed the brook with the water half up my legs, the other horſe followed without difficulty.   This done, I would have ſaluted the ladies, and gone off like a booby : they ſpoke ſoftly to each other, and Miſs G***, addreſſing her-ſelf to me, No, no, ſaid ſhe, you muſt not
                                                leave

leave us in that manner. You have wetted yourfelf to ferve us, and we ought, in confcience,
to take care and dry you : pleafe to come with
us, we take you prifoner.   My heart beat;
I looked at Mifs Galley.   Yes, yes, faid fhe,
laughing at my bewildered look, prifoner of
war   get up behind her, we'll give an account of you. But, Mifs, I have not the honour
of being known to your mother ;   what will fhe
fay on feeing me there ?   Her mother, replied
Mifs de G***, is not at Toune ; we are alone :
we return to-night, and you fhall come back
with us.

    The effect of electricity is not quicker than
that thefe words had on me.   In leaping on
Mifs de G***'s horfe, I trembled with joy,
and when I was to embrace her to hold myfelf on, my heart beat fo ftrong fhe perceived
it · fhe told me hers beat likewife through fear
of falling, this was, in my pofture, an invi-
tation to verify the affair : I never dared during the whole ride ; my two arms ferved her as
a girdle, extremely tight, but without changing, one moment, their pofition.   Some women who read this would box my ears with
pleafure, and would not be to blame.

    The pleafure of the journey, and thefe
girls chatter, fo much fharpened mine, that
till the evening, and the whole time we were
together, we were never filent a moment.
They made every thing fo agreeable, my
tongue faid as much as my eyes, though not
the fame things.   A few inftants only, whilft
I was alone with one or the other, the converfation was a little embarraffed, but the
                                        abfent

abfent one foon returned, and did not give us time to explain this confufion.

Arrived at Toune, and I well dried, we breakfafted; after which they muft proceed to the important bufinefs of getting the dinner ready. The two young ladies, while cooking, kiffed, now and then, the farmer's children, and the poor fcullion faw it, biting his lips. They had fent provifions from the town, which fufficed to make an exceeding good dinner, particularly in dainties; but, unfortunately, they had forgot the wine. This forgetfulnefs was not furprifing in girls who drank little; but I was forry, for I depended a little on its affiftance to embolden me. They, likewife, were forry for it, and perhaps for the fame reafon; but I don't think fo. Their lively and charming mirth was innocence itfelf, befides, what could they have done with me between them? They fent for wine every where: none was to be had; fo fober and poor are thefe peafants. As they remarked to me their uneafinefs at it, I told them not to give themfelves the leaft trouble about it; that they had no occafion for wine to make me drunk. This was the only gallantry I dared pronounce the whole day; however, I believe the rogues faw plainly this gallantry was a truth.

We dined in the farmer's kitchen; the two friends fat on benches which were on each fide the table, and their vifitor between them on a three-legg'd ftool. What a dinner! What a remembrance full of charms! How, when we can, at fo trifling an expence, tafte pleafures fo pure and

and fo real, want to feek others ! Never was
dinner at the Mad-houfe of Paris to be compared to this meal ; I don't mean for mirth
only, for pleafing joy, but I mean for fenfuality.

After dinner we thought of œconomy Inftead of taking the coffee that remained at
breakfaft, we kept it for the afternoon, with
cream and cakes they had brought from town ;
and to keep our appetite fharp, we went to
finifh our defert on cherries in the orchard. I
got up the trees, from whence I threw them
clufters, whofe ftones they returned through
the branches   Once Mifs Galley holding her
apron forward, and her head backward, ftood
fo fair, and I aimed fo well, I caufed a bunch
to drop on her neck; at which fhe laughed.
Said I to myfelf, Why are not my lips cherries ? How readily would I throw them there
likewife !

The day paffed thus in romping with the
greateft liberty, and always with the greateft
decency. Not one equivocal word, not one
free expreffion ; we did not impofe this decency on ourfelves ; it came of itfelf ; we followed the manner our heart taught us. In fine,
my modefty, others will fay my ftupidity, was
fuch, that the greateft liberty that efcaped me
was kiffing, once, Mifs Galley's hand. It is
true, the circumftance made this trifling favour valuable. We were alone, I breathed
with difficulty ; her eyes were turned to the
ground. My lips, inftead of feeking words,
refolved to fix on her hand, which fhe gently
drew away, after it was kiffed, with a look
which

which was not an angry one. I don't know what I should have said to her. her friend came in, and I thought her ugly at that instant.

In fine, they remembered, that, if they staid too late, the city gates would be shut. We had only time sufficient to get in by daylight, and hasted to set off, in distributing ourselves as we came. Had I dared, I had transposed this order; for the look from Miss Galley had greatly inflamed me; but I could say nothing, and she could not propose it. On our march we said the day was to blame to end; but, far from complaining of its shortness, we saw we had found the secret of prolonging it by every amusement we were able to invent.

I left them near the place they had taken me up. With what regret did we separate! With what pleasure did we plan another interview! Twelve hours spent together were worth ages of familiarity. The sweet recollection of this day could never torture the hearts of these amiable girls; the tender harmony which reigned amongst us three, was equal to livelier pleasures, and could not have subsisted with them: our fondness for each other was without mystery or disgrace, and we wanted to retain this fondness for ever. Innocence of manners has its sensuality, which is at least of a price with the other, because it has no void, and acts continually. For my part, I know that the remembrance of so delightful a day charms me more, comes back again more to my

heart,

heart, than that of any pleafures I ever tafted. I did not well know what I wanted of thefe two charming girls, but each very much engaged me. I do not fay, that, had I been mafter in this bufinefs, my heart would have been divided, I was fenfible of a preference. I had been happy in having Mifs de G*** for a miftrefs; but if I had had my choice, I fhould have liked her better as a confident. Be that as it may, it feemed, on quitting them, I could not live without one or the other. Who would think I fhould never fee them more, and that here ended our ephemeral amours?

Thofe who read this will not fail to laugh at my gallant adventures, on remarking, that, after many preliminaries, the moft advanced ended in a kifs of the hand. Oh readers, you may miftake! I have, perhaps, had more pleafure in my amours in ending at this kiffed hand, than you will ever have in beginning at leaft there.

Venture, who went very late to bed the night before, came in a little after me. This once I did not fee him with the fame pleafure as ufual; I took care not to tell him how I had paffed the day. The young ladies fpoke of him with little efteem, and feemed difcontented at my being in fo bad hands, this hurt him with me · befides, every thing which diverted me from them muft be difagreeable to me. However, he foon recalled me to him and myfelf by talking of my fituation. It was too critical to laft. Though I fpent very little, my little favings were exhaufted; I was without refources.

No

No news of Mamma; I knew not what to do, and I felt a cruel heart-breaking at seeing Miss Galley's friend reduced to beggary.

Venture told me he had spoke of me to the Chief Justice; that he would take me there to dinner on the morrow; that he was a man who could do me service; besides, an honest man in his way, a man of sense and letters, a very agreeable man in conversation, who had talents and favoured them; then mixing, as usual, the most trifling frivolousness with the most serious affairs, he shewed me a pretty couplet from Paris, to the air of an opera of Mouret, acted at that time. This couplet so much pleased M. Simon, (the Chief Justice's name,) he wanted to compose another in answer, to the same air: he told Venture to compose one likewise; he was so taken with his folly, as to make me compose a third, in order, says he, that they may see couplets arrive the next day, like the sequel of a comic romance.

At night, not being able to sleep, I composed, as well as I could, my couplet: for the first verses I had made, they were passable, better even, or at least with more taste, than I should have made them in the evening; the subject running on a very feeling situation, to which my heart was already much disposed. In the morning I shewed my couplet to Venture, who, thinking it pretty, put it into his pocket, without telling me whether he had composed his or not. We went to dinner at M. Simon's, who received us well. The conversation was agreeable; it could not fail where two men of sense were met, who had edi-

edified by reading. As for me, I acted my part; I listened and said nothing. Neither of them talked of couplets, I said nothing of them neither; and never, that I heard, was any mention made of mine.

M. Simon seemed satisfied with my appearance: it was nearly the whole he saw of me during this interview. He had seen me, several times, at Madam de Warens's, without taking much notice of me · so that from this dinner I must date his acquaintance, which was of no service to me as to the object that caused it, but from which I, afterwards, drew other advantages, which recal his memory with pleasure.

I should be wrong in not speaking of his person, which could not be guessed from his quality of magistrate, and the learning on which he piqued himself. The Lord Chief Justice Simon was not, assuredly, two feet high : his legs straight, small, and even pretty long, had they been perpendicular ; but they stood stretched like a pair of compasses widely opened. His body was not only short, but thin, and in every sense of a most inconceivable smallness He must appear like a grasshopper when naked. His head, of a natural size, with a face well formed, a noble air, pretty good eyes, seemed a false one planted on a stump. He might have spared the expence of dress , for his large periwig alone covered him from top to toe

He had two voices quite different, which incessantly mixed in his conversation, with a contrast at first extremely pleasing, but soon became

came as difagreeable. One grave and fonorous; this was, if I may fay fo, the voice of his head; the other, fharp and piercing, was the voice of his body. Whenever he took care to fpeak with compofure, and governed his breath, he could always fpeak with his coarfe voice; but, the leaft heated, and if a higher accent caught him, this accent became like the whiftling of a key, and he had the greateft trouble in the world to come to his bafs again.

With the figure I have juft drawn, and which I have not exaggerated, M. Simon was a courtier, always ready with his amorous difcourfes, and carried even to coquettry his attention to his perfon.   As he fought his advantages, he the more readily gave audiences in bed; for when a good head was perceived on the pillow, no one imagined there was nothing more.   This fometimes gave rife to fcenes which I am certain all Annecy ftill remembers.

One morning waiting in his bed, or rather on his bed, the arrival of fome people who had fuits at law, in a beautiful night-cap, very fine and white, garnifhed with two large knots of rofe-coloured ribband, a countryman comes in, taps at the door. The maid was gone out.   My Lord Chief Juftice, hearing it increafe, cries, Come in· and this, fpoken a little too quick, fhot from his fhrill voice.   The man goes in, and examines from whence came the woman's voice, and perceiving in the bed a woman's cap and a topknot, he was going out again, afking the lady
a thou-

a thoufand pardons. M. Simon grows angry, and cries fo much the fhriller. The country-man, confirmed in his idea, and thinking himfelf infulted, returns it, telling him, fhe is nothing but a proftitute, and that the Lord Chief Juftice does not fet good examples in his houfe. The Juftice, in fury, and having no other arms than his chamber-pot, was going to throw it at the poor man's head, when his maid came in.

This little dwarf, fo difgraced by nature in his body, was amply rewarded by a well-endowed mind. it was naturally agreeable, and he had taken care to adorn it. Though he was, as was faid, a very great lawyer, he was not fond of his bufinefs. He had taken a turn to polite literature, and had fucceeded. He had particularly laid hold of that fuperficial brilliancy, that airinefs, which fpreads delights in fociety, even with women. He had got by heart all the little ftrokes of the *Ana*, and fuch like. he had the art of making the moft of them, in telling to advantage, with myftery, and as the anecdote of the evening, that which happened fixty years ago. He knew mufic, and fung agreeably with his man's voice. in fine, he had many pretty talents for a magiftrate. By dint of cajoling the ladies of Annecy, he was in favour with them; they had him at their tail like a little monkey He pretended even to fortunes, and that amufed them. A Madam d'Epagny faid, that the greateft favour for him, was to kifs a woman on her knees.

As he knew good authors, and talked much of

of them, his converfation was not only amufing but inftructive In length of time, when
I had taken a turn to ftudy, I cultivated his
acquaintance, and found it very ufeful. I
fometimes went from Chambery to fee him,
where I was at that time. He commended,
animated my emulation, and gave me on my
ftudies good advice, which I have often benefitted by. Unfortunately, this weakly body
contained a tender foul. A few years afterwards he had I don't know what trouble,
which grieved him, and of which he died.
'Twas a lofs; he was certainly a good-natured
little man, whom you began with by laughing
at and ended by efteeming. Though his life
had little to do with mine, as he had given
me ufeful leffons, I thought I might from
gratitude beftow a little corner in remembrance of him.

The moment I was at liberty I ran to the
ftreet where lived Mifs Galley, hoping to fee
fome one go in or out, or opening a window.
Nothing, not even a cat, ftirred, and all the
time I was there they remained as clofe as if
uninhabited The ftreet was little, and no
one ftirring in it. A man was remarked there:
now and then fome one paffed, or came in or
out of the neighbourhood I was much
troubled with my perfon; it feemed to me they
gueffed my bufinefs there, and this idea tortured me: for I always preferred to my pleafures the repofe of thofe who were dear to
me.

In fine, tired of acting the Spanifh lover,
and having no guitar, I refolved to go home,

and write to Miss G***. I had preferred
writing to her acquaintance; but I dared
not, and it was more becoming to write to
her to whom I was indebted for the other's
acquaintance, and with whom I was more
familiar. My letter finished, I carried it to
Miss Giraud's, as was agreed between the
young ladies and me at parting. They themselves gave me this expedient. Miss Giraud was
a quilter, who working, sometimes, at Madam
Galley's, could eafily get in there. The
meffenger did not, however, appear to me
well chofen; but I was fearful, if I started
the least difficulty on this, they would pro-
pofe no other. Befides, I dared not hint that
she would labour in her own behalf. I felt myfelf mortified at her imagining herfelf, for me,
of the fame fex as thofe ladies. In fine, I chofe
that repofitory rather than none, and stuck to
it at all hazards.

At the first word la Giraud guessed me. it
was not very difficult. If a letter to be carried
to a young lady did not fpeak for itfelf, my
fottifh and confufed looks had alone difcovered me. You may think this errand was not
very pleafing to her; she, neverthelefs, undertook it, and executed it faithfully. The next
morning I ran to her houfe and found my anfwer. How did I haften to get out to read and
kifs it at pleafure! That has no occafion to
be told; but the part Miss Giraud acted has,
in whom I found more delicacy and moderation than I expected. Having fenfe enough
to perceive, that, with her thirty-feven, the
eyes of a leveret, a befmeared nofe, fhrill voice,
and

and black fkin, fhe had little chance againft two young graceful girls in all the fplendor of beauty, fhe would neither betray nor ferve them, and chofe, rather, to lofe me than procure me for them.

Merceret, receiving no news of her miftrefs, had fome time intended returning to Fribourg; fhe entirely determined on it. She did more; fhe hinted to her it would not be amifs that fome one conducted her to her father's, and propofed me. Little Merceret, who did not diflike me, thought this idea might be eafily executed. She fpoke to me of it the fame day as an affair fettled; and as I found nothing difpleafing in this manner of difpofing of myfelf, I confented, regarding this journey as an affair of eight days at moft. Giraud, who did not think with me, fettled all. I was obliged to own the ftate of my purfe. They provided for it, Merceret undertook to defray my expences; and to gain on one fide what they loft on the other, at my inftance, it was determined to fend her little luggage forward, and that we fhould go flowly on foot. This was done.

I am forry to make fo many girls in love with me; but as there is no great fubject of vanity in the advantage I took of thefe amours, I think I may tell the truth without fcruple. Merceret, younger and lefs artful than Giraud, never ufed fo ftrong inticements: but fhe imitated my voice, my accent, repeated my words, had for me the attention I fhould have had for her, and always took great care, as fhe was very fearful, that we lay in the fame

cham-

chamber; a matter which feldom refts there, between a young fellow of twenty and a girl of twenty-five.

It refted there, however, this time. My fimplicity was fuch, that, tho' Merceret was not difagreeable, it never came in my head during the whole journey, I don't fay the leaft temptation of gallantry, but even the leaft idea that had any relation to it, and if this idea had ftruck me, I was too ftupid to turn it to advantage. I did not imagine how a girl and a young fellow arrived at lying together, I thought it required ages to prepare this wonderous affair. If poor Merceret in defraying my expences expected fome equivalent, fhe was bit, for we arrived at Fribourg exactly as we fet out from Annecy.

In paffing through Geneva, I went to fee no one; but I almoft fainted on the bridges. I never faw the walls of this happy town, never went into it, without feeling a kind of finking of the heart, which proceeded from tendernefs to excefs. At the fame time the noble image of liberty elevated the mind, that of equality, of union, of mildnefs of manners, touched me even to tears, and infpired a lively forrow at having loft all thefe bleffings. What an error, but ftill how natural! I thought I faw all this in my native country, becaufe I felt it in my heart.

We muft pafs through Nion. What, without feeing my good father! I fhould have died with grief. I left Merceret at the inn, and went to fee him at every hazard. Ah! was I not to blame to dread him? His heart, on

fee-

seeing me, opened to thofe paternal fentiments
with which it was filled What tears were
fhed in our embraces ! He thought, at firft, I
was returned to him. I told him my ftory
and my refolution. He feebly oppofed it.
He fhewed me the dangers to which I expofed
myfelf, and told me the leaft follies were beft.
As to the reft, he was not the leaft tempted
to retain me by force, and in that I think
he was right; but it is certain he did not,
to recal me, do all he might have done, whether he judged from the fteps I had taken I
fhould not have returned, whether he was
puzzled to know, at my age, what to do with
me. I have fince learnt he had an opinion of
my travelling companion, very unjuft and
very far f om truth, but, however, natural
enough. My mother-in-law, a good woman,
a little fweetening, pretended to oblige me
to fup there. I did not ftay, but I told them
I intended to ftay longer with them on my
return, and left them, as a depofit, my little
bundle I had fent by the boat, and which in-
cumbered me The next morning I fet off
early, very happy to have feen my father, and
to have dared to do my duty.

We happily arrived at Fribourg. Towards
the end of the journey, the officioufnefs of
Mifs Merceret decreafed a little. After our
arrival, fhe fhewed me nothing but coolnefs,
and her father, who did not fwim in opulence,
did not give me a very good reception ; I went
to lodge at a public-houfe. I returned to fee
them the next day ; they offered me a dinner,
I accepted it. We feparated with dry eyes ;

I re-

I returned at night to my lodging houſe, and left the place two days after my arrival, without well knowing which way I intended to go.

Here is another circumſtance of my life, where Providence offered me preciſely what I wanted to ſee happy days. Merceret was a very good girl, not brilliant or handſome, but ſhe was not ugly; not paſſionate; a reaſonable girl, except a few trifling humours, which went off with a cry, and never had any outrageous effects. She had a real inclination to me, I might have married her without trouble, and followed the trade of her father. My taſte for muſic would have made me love her. I ſhould have ſettled at Fribourg, a ſmall city, not pretty, but inhabited by very good people. I ſhould have, without doubt, miſſed a deal of pleaſure, but I ſhould have lived in peace to my laſt hour; and I ought to know, better than any one, I ſhould not have heſitated at this bargain.

I returned, not to Nion, but to Lauſanne. I wanted to have a thorough view of the beautiful lake, which is ſeen there in its utmoſt extent. The greateſt part of my ſecret determined motives have not been ſolider. Diſtant views are ſeldom powerful enough to make me act. The uncertainty of future times has always made me regard projects of long execution as the lures of deceit. I give into hope like another, provided it coſts me nothing to entertain it, but if it requires a long and painful attendance, I have done with it. The leaſt trifling pleaſure within
my

my reach tempts me more than the joys of Paradise. I except, however, the pleasures which are followed by pain. those do not tempt me, because I love pure enjoyments, and we never have them so when we know we prepare for repentance.

It was necessary I should arrive somewhere, and the nearest place was the best; for, having lost my road, I found I was in the evening at Moudon, where I spent the little I had left, except ten creutzers, which went the next day at dinner. and coming in the evening to a little village near Lausanne, I went into a public-house without a sous to pay my lodging, and without knowing what would become of me. I was very hungry; I put on a good face, and asked for supper as if I had wherewithal to pay for it. I went to bed without thinking of any thing; I slept soundly, and having breakfasted in the morning, and reckoned with the landlord, I wanted, for seven batz, which my expences amounted to, to leave my waistcoat in pledge. This honest man refused it: he told me, that, thanks to God, he had never stripped any one; that he would not begin for seven batz; that I might keep my waistcoat, and pay him when I could. I was touched with his goodness; but less than I ought to have been, and have been since on its remembrance. It was not long before I sent him his money, with thanks, by a safe hand, but fifteen years afterwards, returning from Italy by way of Lausanne, I was extremely sorry to have forgot the name of the house and the landlord: I should have gone to see

him:

him : it would have given me great pleasure to have reminded him of his charity, and to prove to him it was not badly placed. Services, more important, without doubt, but rendered with more ostentation, did not appear to me so worthy acknowledgment, as the humanity, simple and without parade, of this honest man.

In drawing near Lausanne, I mused on the distress I was in, and the means of extricating myself without acquainting my mother-in-law of my misery; and I compared myself in this walking pilgrimage to my friend Venture on his arrival at Annecy. I was so heated with this idea, that, without thinking I had neither his gentility, nor his talents, I took it in my head to act at Lausanne the little Venture, to teach music I knew nothing of, and to call myself of Paris, where I had never been. In consequence of this noble project, as there was no company where I could act the vicar, and that besides I took care not to run myself amongst those of the art, I began to inform myself of some public-house where one could be well served at a cheap rate. I was directed to one Perrotet, who took boarders. This Perrotet happened to be one of the best men in the world, and received me well. I told him over all my pretty lies as I had prepared them. He promised to speak of me, and endeavour to procure me some pupils he told me he should not ask me for money until I had earned it His board was five white crowns, this was little for the things, but a great deal for me. He advised me to begin by the half-board, which consisted at dinner of

of good foup and no more, but a plentiful
fupper. I agreed. This poor Perrotet advanced
me all thefe things with all the good-nature
poffible, and fpared no pains to ferve me.

How is it, that, having met with fo many
good people in my youth, I find fo few in an
advanced age: is their race extinct? No;
but the rank in which I am obliged to feek
them now, is not that I found them in then.
Amongft the people, where the great paffions
declare themfelves but by intervals, the feelings of nature make themfelves oftener heard:
in more elevated fituations they are abfolutely
ftifled, and, under the mafk of fentiment, it
is only intereft or vanity which fpeaks.

I wrote from Laufanne to my father, who
fent my bundle, and wrote me excellent inftruction I ought to have made better ufe
of. I have already noted inftants of incon-
ceiveable delirium when I was no longer myfelf. Here is another the moft remarkable.
To comprehend to what a point my brain
was turned at that time, and to what degree
I was, as one may fay, *venturized*, it will be
only neceffary to fhew how many extravagancies I gave into at one and the fame time.
I am a finging-mafter, without knowing how
to read a tune, for, had I benefitted of the
fix months I paffed with le Maitre, they could
not have fufficed. befides this, I was taught
by a mafter, which was to me enough to learn
indifferently. A Parifian of Geneva, and a
catholic in a proteftant country, I thought I
might change my name as well as my religion
and my country. I always followed my grand

K 5   model

model as near as I could. He called himfelf
Venture de Velleneuve, and I turned the ana-
gram of the name of Roufleau into that of
Vauffore, and called myfelf Vauffore de Villeneuve. Venture could compofe, tho' he had
faid nothing of it; and I, who knew nothing
of it, boafted to all the world I underftood it
very well; and, without being able to prick
the commoneft fong, gave out I was a com-
pofer. This is not all: having been prefented
to Monfieur de Treytorens, profeffor in law,
who was fond of mufic, and had concerts at his
houfe, I muft give him a fample of my talents,
and fet about compofing a piece for his concert, with as much effrontery as if I had underftood it.   I had the conftancy to labour,
a fortnight, at this charming work, to write
it fair, to draw out the parts, and diftribute
them with as much affurance as you would
have given out a mafter-piece of harmony.
In fine, that which will be fcarcely believed,
but which is certain, worthily to crown this
fublime production, I added at the end a pretty minuet, fung in the ftreets, and which
perhaps every one ftill recollects, to thefe
words, formerly fo well known:

> Quel caprice !
> Quelle injuftice !
> Quoi, ta Clarice
> Trahiroit tes feux ? &c.

Venture had taught me this air, with the
bafs, to other words, by which aid I had retained it.   I therefore added, at the end of
my compofition, this minuet and his bafs,
suppreffing

suppreſſing the words, and gave them out as my own, as reſolutely as if I had talked to the inhabitants of the moon.

They aſſemble to execute my piece; I explain to each one the motion, manner of execution, and references to parts: I had enough to do. They accord for five or ſix minutes, which to me were five or ſix ages. In fine, every thing ready, I ſtrike, with a fine roll of paper, my magiſterial deſk five or ſix ſtrokes of *take care*. There is a ſilence, I gravely begin to beat time, they begin . . . . no, ſince a French opera exiſts, in your life did you ever hear ſuch horrid muſic. Whatever they had thought of my pretended talents, the effect was worſe than they ſeemed to expect. The muſicians were ſtifled with laughter; the auditors ſtared, and would have been glad to have ſtopped their ears; but there was no poſſibility. My butchers of performers, who were determined to have fun enough, continued ſcraping ſo as to pierce the tympanum of him who was born deaf. I had conſtancy enough to continue at the ſame rate, ſweating, it is true, large drops, but, kept to it by ſhame, not daring to run off, I remained nailed there. For my comfort, I heard around me the company whiſpering in each other's ear, or rather in mine, This is inſupportable! another ſays, What outrageous muſic! another, What a deviliſh catterwauling! Poor Jean-Jacques, in this cruel moment you had no great hopes, that there might come a day, when, before the King of France and his whole Court, your ſounds would excite whiſpers of ſurpriſe and applauſe,

K 6

and

and that, in every box around you, the moſt amiable women would ſay to themſelves in a low voice, What delightful ſounds ! What enchanting muſic ! Every note reaches the heart.

But it was the minuet brought them back to good humour. They had ſcarcely played a meaſure or two, when I heard burſtings of laughter from every part of the room. Every one complimented me on my taſte for muſic : they aſſured me this minuet would make me talked of, and that I merited praiſe from every quarter of the globe. It is unneceſſary to paint my feelings, or to own I well deſerved them.

The next day one of my ſymphoniſts, named Lutold, came to ſee me ; he had good nature enough not to compliment me on my ſucceſs. The deep ſenſe of my impertinence, the ſhame, grief, deſpair on the ſituation to which I was reduced, the impoſſibility of keeping my troubled heart ſhut, cauſed me to open it to him ; I gave a looſe to tears, and, inſtead of contenting myſelf with owning my ignorance, I told him every thing, begging him to keep the ſecret, which he promiſed, and which he kept as every one may gueſs. The ſame evening all Lauſanne knew who I was, but, what was moſt remarkable, nobody would ſeem to know it, not even the good-natured Perrotet, who did not on that account diſcontinue lodging and boarding me.

I lived, but very ſorrowfully. The effects of ſuch a beginning did not render Lauſanne a very agreeable reſidence to me. Pupils did
not

not come in crowds ; not a fingle female one,
and no one of the city. I had only two or
three big Germans, as ftupid as I was ignorant,
who tired me to death, and who, under my
hands, did not become the greateft of muficians. I was fent for to one houfe only, where
a little ferpent of a girl took pleafure in fhewing me a deal of mufic of which I could not read
a fingle note, and which fhe was malicious
enough to fing afterwards to her mafter, to
fhew him how it fhould be executed. I was fo
little capable of reading an air on firft fight,
that, in the brilliant concert I have fpoken of, it
was not in my power to follow the execution
a moment, to know whether what I had under my eye was well played, and which I
myfelf had compofed.

Amidft fo many mortifications, I had the
fweet confolation of receiving, from time to
time, letters from my two charming acquaintances.   I have always found a con-
foling virtue in the fair, and nothing fo much
foftens my afflictions in difgrace, as to fee they
affect an amiable perfon.   This correfpon-
dence ceafed, however, foon afterwards, and
was never renewed , but that was my fault. In
changing my abode, I neglected fending my
direction ; and forced, by neceffity, to think
continually of myfelf, I very foon forgot
them.

It is long fince I mentioned my poor
Mamma, but if it is thought I had forgot her,
'tis a miftake.   I never ceafed thinking of
her, and wifhing to find her again, not to
fupply the wants of a fubfiftence, but thofe

of

of my heart   My affection for her, however
lively, however tender, did not prevent me
from loving others; but not in the same manner.   All equally owed my passion to their
charms, but it solely depended on those of
others, and had not survived them; but
Mamma might grow old and ugly without my
loving her less tenderly.   My heart had entirely transmitted to her person the homage
it immediately paid her beauty, and whatever
change she suffered, provided it was still herself, my feelings could never change. I know I
owed her gratitude; but I really did not think
of it.   Whatever she had done, or had not
done for me, it would have been the same. I
did not love her from duty, interest, or con-
venience; I loved her because I was born
to love her.   When I became amorous of
another, it caused a diversion I own, I thought
less of her: but I thought of her with the
same pleasure; and never, amorous or not,
did I think of her without feeling that there
was no true happiness for me in this life, so
long as I should be separated from her.

'Though I had so long been without news of
her, I never imagined I had quite lost her, or
that she could have forgot me. I said to myself,
she will know, sooner or later, that I am
wandering about, and will let me know she
is alive, I shall find her again, I am sure of it.
In the mean while it was a comfort to me to
be in her country, to pass down those streets
she had passed, before those houses she had
lived in, and the whole through mere con-
jecture; for one of my stupid humours was
that

that of not daring to inform myfelf of her,
or to pronounce her name without the moſt
abſolute neceſſity. It ſeemed to me, that, in
naming her, I ſaid all ſhe inſpired me with,
that my lips revealed the ſecret of my heart,
and that I in ſome ſort expoſed her. I believe
there was in all this a mixture of fear leſt
ſome one ſhould ſpeak ill of her. Much had
been ſaid of her proceedings, and ſomething
of her conduct. Fearing they might not ſay of
her what I could wiſh to hear, I rather choſe
they ſhould not talk about her.

As my pupils did not greatly employ me,
and her city was but four leagues from Lauſanne, I took a turn there of three or four
days; during this time, the moſt agreeable
perturbation never left me. The aſpect of
the lake of Geneva, and its admirable borders,
had always, in my eyes, a peculiar attraction
I cannot explain, which proceeds, not only
from the beauty of the proſpect, but from I
don't know what more intereſting which affects and melts me. Every time I approach
the country of Vaud, I feel an impreſſion
compoſed of the remembrance of Madam de
Warens who was born there, my father who
lived there, Miſs de Vulſon who had the firſt
fruits of my heart, of ſeveral pleſing journeys
I made there in my childhood, and, it would
ſeem, of ſome other more ſecret and more
powerful cauſe than all theſe. When the ardent deſire of the mild and happy life for which
I was born, returns to fire my imagination, 'tis
always in the country of Vaud, near the lake,
in delightful fields, it fixes. I muſt abſolutely
have

have an orchard on the borders of this lake and
no other, I muft have a friend to be depended
on, an amiable woman, a cow, and a little
boat. I fhall never enjoy perfect happinefs on
earth till I have thefe. I laugh at the fimplicity with which I have feveral times gone into
this country folely to find this imaginary blefI-
ing I was always furprifed to find the inhabitants, particularly the women, of a quite
different character to thofe I fought. How
different that appeared to me! The country
and the people who cover it never feemed to
me made for each other.

In this journey to Vevav, in walking along
thefe beautiful banks, I abandoned myfelf to the
gentleft melancholy. My heart launched with
eagernefs into a thoufand innocent pleafures;
I was moved, I fighed, and fhed tears like a
child. How many times, ftopping to cry
with more eafe, feated on a large ftone, have
I not been amufed, by feeing my tears drop
into the ftream?

At Vevay I lodged at the Key, and, in the
two days I ftaid there without vifiting any
one, I contracted a fondnefs for this city that
has followed me in all my travels, and which
in fine caufed me to fix there the hero of my
romance. I fhould readily fay to thofe who
have tafte and feelings, Go to Vevay, vifit
the country, examine its pofition, take a turn
on the lake, and fay whether Nature did not
make this beautiful country for a Julia, for a
Claire, and for a St. Preux; but don't feek
them there. I return to my hiftory.

As I was a catholic, and owned it, I followed

ed without myftery or fcruple the doctrine I
had embraced. On Sundays, in fine weather,
I went to mafs at Affans, two leagues from
Laufanne. I generally took this trip with
other catholics, particularly a Parifian em-
broiderer, whofe name I have forgot. He
was not fuch a Parifian as myfelf, but a Parifian of Paris, one of God Almighty's arch
Parifians, as good-natured as a Champenois.
He was fo fond of his country he would not
doubt I was of it, for fear of lofing an opportunity of talking of it. M. de Crouzas,
lieutenant of the bailiwic, had a gardener, likewife from Paris; but lefs complaifant, and who
thought the glory of his country queftioned in
daring to fay you were of it, when you had not
that honour. He queftioned me as a man fure
of being caught, and then fmiled malicioufly.
He afked me, once, what there was remarkable at the new market? I was loft, as you
may imagine. Having lived twenty years at
Paris, I ought at prefent to know this city.
If, however, I was now afked a like queftion,
I fhould be no lefs troubled to anfwer, and by
this difficulty it might be equally concluded I
had never been at Paris. So much, even though
you meet truth, is one fubject to build on falfe
principles !

I cannot exactly fay how long I ftaid at
Laufanne I did not take from this city any
thing worthy recollection I only know, that,
not finding a livelihood, I went from thence
to Neufchatel, and paffed the winter. I fucceeded better in this laft city, I had fome pupils, and gained enough to pay off my good
friend

friend Perrotet, who had faithfully sent my bundle, though I was confiderably in his debt.

I infenfibly learnt mufic in teaching it. I lived happy enough, a reafonable man had been fatisfied. but my uneafy mind wanted fomething more. On Sundays and holidays, when at liberty, I ran over the fields and woods of the environs, continually wandering, mufing, fighing, and, once out of the city, never came in till evening. One day, being at Boudry, I went to a public-houfe to dine I faw there a man with a long beard, a violet-coloured coat in the Greek tafte, a furred cap, a noble air and garb, and who had often much difficulty to make himfelf underftood, fpeaking but a gibberifh almoft unintelligible, that refembled, however, Italian more than any other language. I underftood nearly all he faid, and I was the only one, he could exprefs himfelf only by figns to the landlord and the country-people. I fpoke a few words of Italian to him which he perfectly underftood; he got up and embraced me with tranfport. The connection was foon made, a d from that inftant I ferved him as interpreter. He had a good dinner; mine was worfe than indifferent: he invited me to his table, I made little ceremony. By drinking and talking we began to be familiar, and at the end of the repaft we were infeparable. He told me he was a Greek prelate, and arch mendicant of Jerufalem; that he was commanded to make a gathering in Europe for repairing the Holy Sepulchre. He fhewed me beautiful patents from the Czarina and the Emperor;

Emperor; he had some from many other Sovereigns. He was well enough satisfied with what he had already got together, but he had met incredible difficulties in Germany, not understanding a word of German, Latin, or French, and reduced to his Greek, Turkish, and the language of the Franks, as his whole resource, which procured him little in the country he was just beginning on. He proposed my accompanying him as secretary and interpreter. Though I had a smart violet coat, lately purchased, which squared pretty well with my new employment, I had so shabby a look he thought me easily gained; he was not mistaken. Our agreement was soon made; I asked nothing, he promised much. Without security, without bond, without acquaintance, I submit to be conducted by him, and the very next morning here I go for Jerusalem.

We began our tour by the canton of Fribourg, where he did little. The episcopal dignity could not admit of acting the beggar, and gather of individuals; but we presented his commission to the Senate, who gave him a trifling sum. From thence we went to Berne. We lodged at the Falcon, at that time a good inn, where good company were found. There were many people at table, and it was well served. I had long fared very poorly; I had occasion enough to renew myself I had the opportunity, and made good use of it. The arch-mendicant himself was very good company, fond enough of a good table, gay, conversed well with those who understood him, not wanting in certain sciences, and adapting

his

his Greek erudition agreeably enough. One
day, cracking nuts at the defert, he cut his
finger very deep; and as the blood gufhed out
in abundance, he held up his finger to the
company, and fays with a laugh: *Miratė, Sig-
nori, quefto e fangue Pelafgo.*

At Berne my functions were not ufelefs to
him, and I did much better than I expected.
I was much more courageous, and fpoke
better than I fhould have done for myfelf.
Things did not pafs fo fimply as at Fribourg.
Long and frequent conferences with the
principal of the ftate, and the examination
of his titles, were not the work of a day.
At laft, every hing being fettled, he was admitted to an audience of the Senate. I went
with him as his interpreter, and was commanded to fpeak. I did not expect any thing
lefs. it d d not come into my head, that, after
having had long conferred with the members
feparately, the affembly muft be addreffed as
if nothing had been faid. Judge of my embar-
raffment! For fo bafhful a man to fpeak, not
only in public, but before the Senate of Berne,
and fpeak extempore, without having had a
fingle minute to prepare myfelf; this was
enough to annihilate me. I was not even
intimidaed. I reprefent fuccinctly and clearly
the arch-mendicant's commiffion. I praifed
the piety of thofe princes who had contributed
to the gathering he was come to make.
Sharpening with emulation that of their Excell-
encies, I faid, no lefs could be expected from
their accuftomed munificence; and then endeavouring to prove this charitable work to be
equally fo for all chriftians without diftinction
of

of sect, I ended by promising the blessings of Heaven to those who should contribute to it. I shall not say my speech had any effect; but 'tis certain it was relished, and that after the audience the arch-mendicant received an honourable present, and more, on the parts of his secretary, compliments, which I had the agreeable office of interpreting, but which I dared not literally render. This is the only time of my life I spoke in public, and before a sovereign, and, perhaps, the only time likewise I spoke boldly and well What difference in the dispositions of the same man ! It is three years since I went to see at Yverdon my old friend M. Roguin.   I received a deputation of thanks for some books I had made a present of to the library of this city.   The Swifs are much for harangues; these gentlemen harangued me   I thought myself obliged to answer, but I was so embarrassed in my answer, and my head was so confused, I stopped short not knowing what to say, and got myself laughed at. Though naturally timid, I have been some times confident in my youth; never in my advanced age.   The more I see of the world, the less I can form myself to its manner.

On leaving Berne, we went to Soleurre; for the design of the arch-mendicant was to take the road of Germany, and return by Hungary or Poland : this was an immense tour; but as in journeying his purse filled rather than emptied, he little dreaded a winding course.   For my part, who was almost as much pleased on horseback as on foot, I desired no

bet◆

better than thus to travel my whole life-time;
but it was written I fhould not go fo far.

The firft thing we did on our arrival at
Solcurre, was to pay our refpects to theAmbaf-
fador of France. Unfortunately for our bifhop,
the Ambaffador was the Marquis of Bonac,
who had been Ambaffador at the Port, and
who muft be well acquainted with every thing
regarding the Holy Sepulchre. The arch-mendicant had an audience of a quarter of an hour
where I was not admitted, as the Ambaffador
underftood the Franks language, and fpoke
Italian at leaft as well as I. On my Greek's
departure I was following him; I was ftopped:
it was my turn. Having paffed as a Parifian,
I was, as fuch, under the jurifdiction of his
Excellency. He afked me who I was, exhort-
ing me to tell the truth, I promifed it, on
afking a private audience, which was granted. The Ambaffador took me to his clofet,
and fhut the door, and there, throwing myfelf at his feet, I kept my word. I had
not faid lefs, though I had promifed nothing;
for a continual inclination to difclofe my heart
brings every inftant my thoughts on my lips,
and having opened myfelf without releive to
the mufician Lutold, I had no occafion for
any myftery to the Marquis of Bonac. He
was fo fatisfied with my ftory, and the effufion
of heart which he faw accompanied it, he
took me by the hand, led me to the Ambaffa-
drefs, and introduced me to her, in giving an
abridgment of my recital. Madam de Bonac
received me with kindnefs, and faid they muft
not

not let me go with this Greek monk. It was
determined I fhould remain at the hotel until
they faw what might be done with me. I
wanted to go take my leave of my poor arch-
mendicant, for whom I had conceived a friendfhip : it was not permitted. They fent him
notice of my arreft, and in a quarter of an
hour I faw my little bundle brought in. M.
de la Martiniere, fecretary to the embaffy, had
in fome fort the care of me. In conducting
me to the room intended for me, he faid to
me, This room was occupied under the Count
Du Luc, by a celebrated man of the fame
name as yourfelf. It depends on you to replace
him in every manner, that it may be one day faid,
Roufleau the Firft, Roufleau the Second. This
conformity, which at that time I had little
hopes of, had lefs flattered my wifhes, had I
been able to forefee how dear I fhould one day
pay for it.

M. de la Martiniere's words excited my
curiofity. I read the works of him whofe
room I occupied, and, on the compliment
paid me, imagining I had a tafte for poefy,
I made for my trial a canta'a in praife of
Madam de Bonac. This turn flagged. I
have now and then made indifferent verfe ;
'tis a good exercife enough to break one's felf
into elegant inverfions, and teach one to write
better profe , but I never found charms fufficient in French poetry to give myfelf entirely
to it.

M. de la Martiniere wanted to fee my ftyle,
and afked me the fame particulars in writing
I had told the Ambaffador. I wrote him a
long

long letter, which I heard was preserved by
M. de Marianne, who was a long while with
the Marquis de Bonac, and who has since
succeeded M. de la Martiniere in M. de Cour-
teilles' embassy I have begged M. deMalesher-
bes to endeavour to procure me a copy of this
letter.   If I get it by him or others, it will
be round in the collection which I intend shall
accompany my Confessions.

The experience I began to have, moderated
by degrees my romantic projects ; and as a
proof, not only I did not fall in love with
Madam de Bonac, but immediately saw I
should do but little in her husband's family. M.
de la Martiniere in place, and M. de Marianne
in survivance, as one may say, left me no farther hopes for my fortune than the place
of under-secretary, which little tempted me.
This was the cause, that, when I was con-
sulted on what I should like, I shewed a great
inclination to go to Paris.   The Ambassador
relished this idea, which tended, at least, to
his getting rid of me.   M. de Merveilleux,
secretary and interpreter to the embassy, said
his friend M. Goddard, a Swiss colonel in the
service of France, wanted some one to be with
his nephew, who entered very young into the
service, and thought I might suit him.   On
this notion, slightly enough taken, my departure was resolved ; and I, who saw a journey in the case, and Paris at the end, was as
joyful as joy could make me.   They gave
me some letters, an hundred livres for my
journey, accompanied by very good advice, and
I set off.

I was

I was on this journey fifteen days, which I may reckon among the happy ones of my life. I had youth, health, money enough, great hopes, travelled on foot and alone. You will be surprised to see me reckon this an advantage, if you were not already familiar with my humour. My pleasing chimeras kept me company, and never did the heat of my imagination give birth to any so magnificent. If I was offered an empty place in a carriage, or that any one accosted me on the road, my temper grew four at seeing my fortune crossed, whose edifice I built up as I walked. This once my notions were martial: I was going to engage to a military man, and become a military man myself; for it was settled I should begin by entering a cadet. I thought I already saw myself in an officer's dress, with a fine white feather in my hat. My heart swelled at this noble idea. I had a little smattering of geometry and fortification; I had an uncle an engineer; I was, in some fort, of the bullet family. My near sight offered a few obstacles, which never troubled me; and I supposed that presence of mind and intrepidity would supply this failing. I had read that Marshal Schomberg was near-sighted; why might not Marshal Rousseau be so? I so heated myself by these follies, I saw nothing but armies, ramparts, gabions, batteries, and myself amidst fire and smoke, coolly giving orders, my spying-glass in my hand However, when I passed through agreeable fields, and saw groves and rivulets, the striking scene drew sighs of sorrow; I felt, amidst all this glory, my heart was not inclined to fo much havock; I returned to my beloved fheep-folds, for ever renouncing the labours of Mars.

How much did the firft fight of Paris bely the idea I had of it! The external decoration I had feen at Turin, the beauty of the ftreets, the fymmetry and fquarenefs of the houfes, induced me to feek at Paris ftill more. I had figured to myfelf a city as beautiful as large, of the moft impofing afpect, where nothing was feen but fuperb ftreets and marble or golden palaces. Coming in at the fuburbs St. Marceau, I faw none but little, dirty, ftinking ftreets, ugly black houfes, the appearance of naftinefs, poverty, beggars, carters, old cloaths botchers, criers of ptifan and old hats. All thefe things ftruck me, at firft, to fuch a degree, that all I have feen at Paris, really magnificent, has not been able to deftroy this firft impreffion, and that there ftill remains a fecret difguft to the refidence of this capital. I can fay the whole time I afterwards remained there, was employed in feeking refources which might enable me to live far from it. Such is the fruit of a too active imagination, which exaggerates beyond the exaggerations of mankind, and always fees more in a thing than has been heard. I had heard Paris fo much boafted of, I looked on it like ancient Babylon, from which I fhould, perhaps, have found full as much to deduct, had I feen it, from the picture I had drawn of it. The fame thing happened to me at the opera, where I haftened to go the morrow of my arrival: the fame afterwards happened at Verfailles;

failles, after that, likewise, on feeing the fea; and the fame thing will always happen to me, on feeing any thing too much extolled; for it is impoffible to mankind, and difficult to Nature itfelf, to furpafs the richnefs of my imagination.

From the manner I was received by all thofe for whom I had letters, I thought my fortune made. Him I was moft recommended to, and leaft careffed by, was M. de Surbeck, retired from the fervice, and living philofophically at Bagneux, where I went feveral times to fee him, without his once offering me even a glafs of water. I was better received by Madam de Merveilleux, fifter-in-law to the interpreter, and by his nephew, an officer in the guards. The mother and fon not only received me well, but offered me their table, of which I often benefitted during my ftay at Paris. Madam de Merveilleux appeared to me to have been handfome; her hair was a beautiful black, and formed, in the old fashion, ringlets on her forehead. That which does not perifh with beauty ftill remained, an agreeable mind. She feemed pleafed with mine, and did all in her power to ferve me; but no one feconded her, and I was foon undeceived on all this great intereft they appeared to take in my behalf. I muft, however, do the French juftice; they do not fmother you with proteftations, as is faid of them; and thofe they make are almoft always fincere; but they have a manner of interefting themfelves in your favour, which deceives you more than words. The coarfe compliments of the Swifs

can

can impofe on fools only. The French manners are more feducing, only becaufe they
are more fimple; you think they don't tell
you all they intend to do for you, to furprife
you more agreeably. I fhall go farther: they
are not falfe in their demonftrations; they
are naturally officious, humane, benevolent,
and even, whatever may be faid of it, more
downright than any other nation; but they
are light and airy. They have, in effect, the fentiment they exprefs; but this fentiment goes off
as it came. While fpeaking to you, they are
full of you; go out of their fight, they have
forgot you. Nothing is permanent in them;
every thing with them lafts but a moment.

I was therefore flattered much, ferved little.
The Colonel Godard, whofe nephew I was
to be with, feeing my diftrefs, and although
rolling in riches, wanted me for nothing. He
pretended that I fhould be with his nephew,
a kind of valet without wages rather than as
a real tutor. Continually engaged with him,
and by that difpenfed from duty, I muft live
on my cadet's pay, that is, a foldier's; it was
with trouble he confented to give me a uniform; he had been glad to put me off with
that of the regiment. Madam de Merveilleux, enraged at his propofals, advifed me
herfelf not to accept them, her fon was of
the fame opinion. Other things were fought,
but nothing found. I began, however, to be in
want; an hundred livres on which I had made
my journey, could not carry me far. Happily,
I received from the Ambaffador a trifling
remittance, which was very ufeful; and I
believe

believe he had not difcarded me, had I had more patience : but to languifh, wait, folicit, are, to me, impoffibilities. I was difcouraged, appeared no more, and all was at an end. I had not forgot my poor Mamma, but how to find her ? where feek her ? Madam de Merveilleux, who knew my ftory, affifted me in the refearch, but long to no purpofe. At laft fhe told me that Madam de Warens had been gone more than two months, but it was not known whether to Savoy or Turin, and that fome faid fhe was returned to Switzerland. Nothing more was neceffary to determine me to follow her, certain, that, wherever fhe might be, I fhould find her in the country much eafier than I could have done at Paris.

Before my departure, I exercifed my new poetical talent, in an epiftle to Colonel Godard, in which I bantered him as well as I could. I fhewed this fcrawl to Madam de Merveilleux, who, inftead of cenfuring me, as fhe ought, laughed heartily at my farcafms, and her fon likewife, who, I believe, did not love M Godard, it muft be owned he was not amiable. I was tempted to fend him my verfes, they encouraged me : I made a parcel of them directed to him ; and, as there was no penny-poft then at Paris, I fent it from Auxerre in paffing through that place. I laugh yet, fometimes, on thinking of the grimaces he muft have made on reading his panegyric, where he was painted ftroke by ftroke. It began thus:

Tu croyois, vieux Penard, qu'une folle manie
D'élever ton neveu m'infpireroit l'envie

This

This little piece, badly compofed in fact, but which did not want falt, and which fhewed a talent for fatire, is neverthelefs the only fatirical work that ever came from my pen. My mind is too little inclined to hatred to glory in this kind of talent; but I fancy you may judge by fome pieces of controverfy, written from time to time, in my defence, that, had I been of a warring humour, my aggreffors had feldom had the laughers on their fide.

What I moft regret in the particulars of my life, which I do not remember, is not having kept a journal of my travels. Never did I think, exift, live, or was myfelf, if I may fay fo, fo much as in thofe I made alone and on foot. Walking has fomething which animates and enlivens my ideas I can fcarcely think when I ftand ftill; my body muft ftir in order to ftir my mind. The view of the country, the fucceffion of agreeable fights, a good air, a good appetite, and good health, I get by walking; the freedom of inns, the diftance of thofe objects which force me to fee fubjection, of every thing which reminds me of my condition, the whole gives a loofe to my foul, gives me more boldnefs of thought, carries me, in a manner, into the immenfity of beings, fo that I combine them, chufe them, appropriate them to my will, without fear or reftraint. I imperioufly difpofe of all Nature: my heart, wandering from object to object, unites, becomes the fame with thofe which engage it, is compaffed about by delightful images, grows drunk with delicious fenfations. If to determine

mine them, I divert myfelf by painting them
in my mind, what vigorous touches, what re-
fplendent colouring, what energy of expreffion do l not give them ! We have, you'll
fay, feen all this in your works, though written
in the decline of life. Oh ! had you known
thofe of the flower of my youth, thofe I made
during my travels, thofe I compofed but never
wrote .... Why, fay you, did you not write
them ? And why write them, I anfwer you ;
why withdraw myfelf from the actual charms
of enjoyment, to tell others I did enjoy ?
What cared I for readers, the public, and the
whole earth, while I was fwimming in the
heavens ? Befides, did I carry ink and pa-
pei ? Had I thought of all thefe things, nothing had ftruck me I did not forefee l fhould
have ideas , they come when they pleafe, not
when I pleafe; they overwhelm me with
number and force. Ten volumes a day had
not fufficed. Where borrow time to write
them ? On arriving I thought of nothing but
a hearty dinner. On departing I thought of
nothing but trudging on. I faw a new Paradife awaited me at the door, I ran off to
catch it.

I never felt all this fo much as in the
journey I am fpeaking of. In coming to
Paris I was confined to ideas relative to the
bufinefs I was going on. I launched into the
career I was going to run, and fhould have run
thro' it with glory enough, but this career was
not that my heart called me to, and real beings prejudiced imaginary ones. Colonel Godard and his nephew made poor figures when

L 4

oppofed

oppofed to a hero like me. Thanks to Heaven! I was now delivered from all thefe obstacles; I could plunge at will into the land of chimeras, for nothing more was feen before me. And I was fo far bewildered in it, I really loft, feveral times, my road. I had been very forry to have gone ftraighter; for finding, at Lyons, I was almoft on earth again, I had been glad never to have reached it.

One day, among others, going on purpofe out of my road, the better to fee a fpot which appeared admir·ble, I was fo delighted with it, and went around it fo often, I entirely loft myfelf. After running backwards and forwards feveral hours in vain, tired and dy.ng of hunger and thirft, I went to a country perfon's, whofe houfe had not a very good appearance, but it was the only one I faw near me. I thought it was as it is at Geneva or Switzerland, where every inhabitant, who could afford it, might exercife hofpitality. I begged this man to let me dine with him for my money. He offered me fome fkimmed milk and coarfe barley bread, and told me 'twas all he had. I drank the milk with pleafure, and eat the bread, ftraw and all; but this was not very ftrengthening to a man-exhaufted with fatigue. The countryman, who examined me, judged of the truth of my ftory by that of my appetite. Having told me that he very well faw * I was a good-natured, honeft young man, who

* It feems I had not, at that time, the phyfiognomy they have fince given me in my portraits.

was

was not come there to betray him, he opened
a little trap-door near the kitchen, went down,
and in an inftant came back with a good houfe-
hold loaf of pure wheat, a gammon of bacon very
enticing, though already cut, and a bottle of
wine, whofe appearance raifed my fpirits more
than all the reft.   An omelet pretty thick was
added to thefe, and I made a dinner fuch as
thofe only who travel on foot were ever acquainted with.   When I offered to pay, his
uneafinefs and fears come on him again, he
would not take my money; he returned it
with extraordinary agitation; and the plea-
fanteft of all was, I could not imagine what
he had to dread.   At laft he pronounced with
trembling thefe terrible words, Officers and
Cellar-rats. He made me underftand that he hid
his wine for fear of the excife, his bread for fear
of the poll-tax, and that he was a ruined man,
had they the leaft doubt but that he was ftarving with hunger.   Every thing he told me on
this fubject, of which I had not the leaft idea,
made an impreffion on me that will never wear
away.   This was the fpring and fource of that
inextinguifhable hatred which hath fince un-
folded itfelf in my heart againft the vexations
the poor people experience, and againft their
oppreffors.   This man, though in eafy cir-
cumftances, dared not eat the bread he had
earned by the fweat of his brow, and could
efcape ruin folely by an appearance of that
want which was feen all around him.   I went
from his houfe with as much indignation as
pity, deploring the fate of thefe beautiful
countries to which Nature has been lavifh in

her

her gifts, only to fall a prey to barbarous publicans.

This is the only thing I diſtinctly remember of all that happened in this journey. I recollect only one thing more, that, in approaching Lyons, I was tempted to prolong my travels by going to ſee the borders of the Lignon: for among the romances I read at my father's, Aſtrea had not been forgotten; it came more frequently to my mind than any other thing. I aſked the road to Forez, and, in chatting with a landlady, ſhe told me it was a rare country for workmen, that it contained many forges, and that good iron work was done there. This encomium at once calmed my romantic curioſity; I did not think proper to go to ſeek Diana's and Silvanus's amidſt a generation of blackſmiths. The good old woman who encouraged me in this manner, certainly took me for a journeyman lockſmith.

I did not quite go to Lyons without ſome view. On my arrival, I went to ſee, at the Chaſottes, Miſs du Châtelet, an acquaintance of Madam de Warens, and for whom ſhe had given me a letter when I came with M. le Maitre; it was, therefore, an acquaintance already made. Miſs du Châtelet told me, that, in fact, her friend had paſſed through Lyons, but ſhe could not tell whether ſhe had continued her road as far as Piedmont, and that ſhe was uncertain herſelf, at her departure, whether or no ſhe ſhould not ſtop in Savoy; that, if I choſe, ſhe would write in order to learn ſomething of her, and that the beſt way

was

was to wait the anſwer at Lyons. I accepted the offer; but dared not tell Miſs du Châtelet a ſpeedy anſwer was neceſſary; and that my little exhauſted purſe did not leave me in a condition to wait long. It was not her bad reception that withheld me. On the contrary, ſhe ſhewed me much kindneſs, and treated me in a ſtyle of equality that diſheartened me from letting her ſee my ſituation, and deſcending from the line of good company to that of a beggar

I think I clearly ſee the agreement of all I have mentioned in this book. I, nevertheleſs, ſeem to recollect, in the ſame interval, another journey to Lyons, whoſe place I cannot fix, and in which I was much ſtraightened: the remembrance of the extremities to which I was reduced, does not contribute to recal it agreeably to my memory. Had I done like ſome others, had I poſſeſſed the talent of borrowing and running in debt at my lodging, I had eaſily got through; but in this my unaptneſs equalled my repugnance; and to imagine the point to which I carried both one and the other, it is ſufficient to know, that, having ſpent almoſt my whole life in hardſhips, and often at the point of wanting bread, it never happened to me, once in my life, to be aſked, by a creditor, for money, without giving it him that inſtant. I never could contract bawling debts, and was always fonder of ſuffering than owing.

To be reduced to lie in the ſtreet was certainly ſuffering, and this happened to me ſeveral times at Lyons. I choſe to employ the

ſew

few halfpence that remained, in paying for bread rather than a lodging; becaufe, after all, I run lefs hazard of dying for want of fleep than bread. It is furprifing, that, in this cruel fituation, I was neither uneafy nor dull. I had not the leaft care for future days. I waited the anfwers Mifs de Châtelet was to receive, lodging in the open air, and fleeping ftretched on the earth, or on a bench, with the fame eafe as on a bed of down. I remember to have paffed even a delightful night out of the city, on a road which borders the Rhône or the Saône, I don't recollect which of the two. Gardens forming terraces bordered the road on the oppofite fide. It had been extremely hot that day; the evening was charming; the dew moiftened the drooping grafs; no wind, a ftill night; the air was frefh, but not cold; the fun being fet had left red vapours in the heavens whofe reflection gave to the water the colour of a rofe; the trees on the terrace were covered with nightingales, who anfwered each other's notes. I walked about in a fort of extacy, giving up my feelings and heart to the enjoyment of the whole, and fighing a little with grief at enjoying it alone. Abforbed in delightful meditation, the night was far advanced before I perceived my lengthened walk had tired my weary limbs. I perceived it at laft. I laid myfelf luxurioufly on the ftep of a fort of niche or falfe door in the terrace walk the canopy of my bed was formed by the tops of trees; a nightingale was precifely over my head, his mufic lulled me afleep: my flumbers were foft, my awaking was more fo. It was broad day. my eyes, on opening, faw water, verdure, and an admirable landfcape. I got up, fhook myfelf, hunger feized me. I made, gayly, the beft of my way towards town, refolved to fpend on a good breakfaft the laft two pieces I had left. I was in fo excellent a humour as to go finging along all the way, and, I alfo remember, I fung a cantata of Batiftin I had by heart, intitled the *Baths of Thomery*. God blefs the good Batiftin and his good cantata, which brought me a better breakfaft than what I expected, and ftill a better dinner, which I did not expect at all. In the height of my walking and finging, I heard fome one behind me. I look round, I fee an Antonine following me, and feeming to liften to me with pleafure. He accofts me, bids me good-morning, and afks if I know mufic? I anfwered, *a little*, to make it believed a great deal. He continues to queftion me. I tell a part of my ftory. He afks me whether I ever copied mufic? Often, fay I, which was true; my beft method of learning was by copying. Well, fays he, come with me; I can employ you a few days, during which time you fhall want nothing, provided you confent to not going out of the room. I willingly acquiefced, and followed him.

This Antonine was named Rolichon, was fond of mufic, underftood it, and fung in little concerts he gave his friends There was nothing in this but innocence and decency, but this tafte degenerated, no doubt, into paffion, of which he was obliged to conceal a part.

He

He conducted me to a little room I occupied, where I found a deal of mufic he had copied. He gave me more to copy, particularly the cantata I fung, and which he intended to fing in a little time. I ftaid there three or four days, copying the whole time I did not eat; for in my life I never was fo hungry or better fed He brought my meals himfelf from the kitchen; they muft have had a good one, if their living was equal to mine. In my days I have not eat with fo much pleafure; and I muft own thefe bits came in the nick of time, for I was as dry as wood I work with nearly as good a heart as I eat, which is not faying à little. It is true I was not fo correct as diligent. Some days after, M. Rolichon, whom I met in the ftreet, told me my parts could not be performed on account of omif- fions, duplications, and tranfpofitions. I muft own I have, in chufing that, chofe the only fcience in the world for which I was leaft calculated. Not but that my notes were good, and that I copied very clean; but the tedouf- nefs of a long job diftracts me fo much, that I fpend more time in fcratching out than in noting; and if I do not ufe the greateft attention in comparing my parts, they always caufe the performance to fail. I, therefore, in endeavouring to do well, did very ill, and to get on quickly, I went crofs. This did not prevent M. Rolichon from treating me well the whole time, and giving me, on leav- ing him, half-a-crown I little deferved, but which fet me quite on foot again; for in a few days after I received news from Mamma,

who

who was at Chambery, and money to carry me
to her: this journey I made with transport. Since
these times my finances have been very low;
but never so as to go without bread. I mention
this period with a heart sensible of the attention of Providence.   It was the last time of
my life I felt hunger and misery.

I staid at Lyons seven or eight days more,
waiting the things which Mamma had desired
Miss du Châtelet to get for her. I attended this
lady more assiduously, during this time, than
before, having the pleasure of talking with her
of her friend, without being any longer taken
off by those cruel reflections on my situation
which forced me to conceal it.   Miss du Châtelet was neither young nor pretty, but she did
not want agreeableness; she was easy and familiar, and her wit gave a price to this familiarity.   She had the faculty of observing morals, which teaches to study mankind, and it
is from her in its first origin I derive this
taste.   She was fond of le Sage's romances,
and particularly Gil Blas, she spoke to me
of it, lent it me, and I read it with pleasure;
but I was not then ripe for this kind of reading : I wanted romances of flighty sentiments.
I thus passed my time at the grate of Miss du
Châtelet with as much pleasure as profit; it is
certain the interesting and sensible conversations
of a woman of merit are more proper to
form a young man, than all the pedantic phi-
losphy of books.   I got acquainted at the
Chasottes with other boarders and their friends;
among others, with a young person of four-
teen, named Miss Serre, to whom I did not,
at

at firft, pay much attention; but whom I grew fond of eight or nine years afterwards, and with reafon; fhe was a charming girl.

Occupied with the expectation of foon feeing again my dear Mamma, I made a little truce with my chimeras; and the true happinefs that awaited me difpenfed me with feeking them in vifions. I not only found her again, but I found with her, and by her means, an agreeable fituation, for fhe wrote me word fhe had got me an occupation fhe hoped would fuit me, without feparating from her. I fpent myfelf in conjectures in guefling what this occupation could be, and it was neceffary to guefs, in fact, in order to meet it exactly. I had money fufficient to travel conveniently. Mifs du Châtelet would have had me taken a horfe, I could not confent, and had reafon on my fide: I had miffed the pleafure of the laft journey on foot I ever made; for I can't call by this name the excurfions I often made round my neighbourhood, when I lived at Motiers

It is a fingular thing, that my imagination never rifes more agreeably than when my condition is the leaft fo; and that, on the contrary, it is lefs fmiling when every thing fmiles around me. My ftubborn head cannot fubmit to things, it can't embellifh, it will create. Real objects are fhewn there at moft but as they are, it can drefs out none but imaginary objects. Would I paint fpring, it muft be in winter; would I defcribe a beautiful landfcape, I muft be fhut up; and I have an hundred times faid, that, if ever they put
me

me into the Baſtille, I ſhould compoſe the
picture of Liberty. On leaving Lyons I ſaw
nothing but future delights ; I was as happy,
and had every reaſon to be ſo, as I was the
reverſe on leaving Paris. I, neverthelefs, had
none of thoſe delightful meditations in this
journey I had in the other. My heart was at
eaſe, and that was all. I drew near that excellent
friend I was going to ſee again with melting
fondneſs. I taſted before-hand, but without
ebriety, the pleaſure of living with her : I always expected it ; it was as if nothing new
had happened. I was diſquieted at what I was
going to do as if it had been very diſquieting.
My ideas were peaceable and mild, not celeſ-
tial and raviſhing. Objects ſtruck my ſight ;
I gave attention to the landſcapes ; I obſerved
the trees, the houſes, the brooks ; I conſider-
ed the croſſing of roads ; I feared loſing myſelf,
but did not. In a word I was no longer in the
Empyreum ; I was ſometimes where I was,
ſometimes where I was going to, never farther.

I am in recounting my travels as I was in
making them: I cannot arrive. My heart
beat when I drew near my dear Mamma, but
I went no faſter for that. I love to walk at
my eaſe, and ſtop when I pleaſe. I love a
ſtrolling life. Make a journey on foot in fine
weather, in a fine country, and an agreeable
object at the end it; this is of all the manners of living the moſt to my taſte. As to the
reſt, 'tis underſtood what I mean by a fine
country. Never a champain country, however fine it may be, appeared ſo in my eyes. I
muſt

muſt have torrents, rocks, fir-trees, gloomy woods, mountains, roads which are rugged to go up or down, precipices on each ſide which affright me. I had this pleaſure and taſted all its delights in approaching Chambery. Not far from a cut mountain, called the Pas-de-l'Echelle, at the bottom of a great road cut through the rock, at a place called Chailles, is a little river, which runs and ſpouts into dreadful abyſſes which it ſeems to have taken thouſands of ages to hollow out. They have bordered the road by a parapet to prevent accidents . by this means I could contemplate the bottom, and make myſelf giddy at my eaſe ; for what is moſt pleaſant in my taſte for ſteep places, is that they make my head run round, and that I am very fond of this turning round, provided I am ſafe. Leaning firmly on the parapet, I advanced my head, and remained there whole hours, perceiving from time to time the froth and the blue water, whoſe roaring I heard amidſt the cries of ravens and birds of prey, which flew from rock to rock, and from thicket to thicket, between ſix and ſeven hundred feet below me. In thoſe places where the deſcent was pretty regular, and the buſhes thin enough to let ſtones paſs, I fetched ſome from a pretty good diſtance, as large as I could carry, piled them on a heap on the parapet, then throwing them one after the other, I was delighted to ſee them roll, bound, and fly into a thouſand pieces before they reached the bottom of the precipice.

Nearer Chambery I had a like ſight in a contrary ſenſe. The road paſſes at the foot of the fineſt

fineſt caſcade I have ever ſeen. The mountain is ſo ſteep, that the water flies off neat,
and falls in the form of an arcade ſo wide that
you can paſs between the caſcade and the rock,
ſometimes without being wetted. But, if you
don't take your meaſures well, you may be taken
in, as I was; for, from the extreme height,
the water divides and falls into a miſt, and
when you approach this cloud a little, without
immediately perceiving you are wet, in an inſtant you are well ſoaked.

I arrive at laſt; I ſee her again. She was
not alone. The Intendant-general was in her
room at the time I came in. Without ſpeaking to me, ſhe takes me by the hand, and preſents me to him with that grace which op
to her every heart. Here he is, Sir, poor youn
fellow; condeſcend to patronize him as long
as he deſerves it ; I am under no apprehenſion
for him the reſt of his life. Then turning to
me, Child, ſays ſhe, you belong to the King:
thank the Intendant, who has provided you
bread. I ſtared without ſpeaking a word, or
without very well knowing what to think:
growing ambition, with a trifling addition,
would have turned my head, and made me
immediately act the little Intendant. My
fortune I found leſs brilliant than I imagined
from this beginning ; but for the preſent it
was a living, which, for me, was a great deal.
This was the affair.

King Victor-Amedee, judging by the fate
of the preceding wars, and by the poſition of
the ancient inheritance of his forefathers, it
might ſome time or other ſlip from him,
thought

thought how he might exhauft it. He had resolved a few years before to tax the nobility, he ordered a general survey of the lands of the whole country, in order, that by laying the real impofition, he might divide it with more equity. This work, begun under the father, was finifhed under the fon. Two or three hundred people, as well furveyors, who were called Geometers, as writers, who were called Secretaries, were employed on this work : it was among thefe laft Mamma had got my name entered. The poft, though not lu-crative, was fufficient to live well upon in that country. The worft was, the employment was only for a term ; but it put one forward in feeking and waiting, and it was by way of forecaft fhe endeavoured to obtain his pri-vate patronage for me, in order to get a more permanent employment when the term of this fhould be expired

I entered into office a few days after my arrival. There was nothing difficult in this work , I was foon mafter of it. 'Twas thus, after four or five years running about in follies and fufferings, fince I left Geneva, I began, for the firft time, to get my bread with credit.

Thefe long particulars of my youth may have appeared very puerile ; I am forry for it. though born a man in many refpects, I was long a child, and am fo yet in many others. I did not promife to hold up to the public a great perfonage , I promifed to paint myfelf fuch as I am, for to know me well in my
ad-

advanced age, it is neceffary to have known me in my youth. As, in general, objects make lefs impreffion on me than their remembrance, and that all my ideas are in refemblance, the firft ftrokes which were engraven on my mind have remained there, and thofe which were imprinted afterwards have rather joined than effaced them. There was a certain fucceffion of affections and ideas which modify thofe which follow, and which it is neceffary to be acquainted with, in order properly to judge of them. I ftrive, every where, to lay the firft caufes quite open, to make you feel the connexion of effects. I want to be able, if I could, by fome means to render my heart tranfparent to the fight of the reader; and this is the reafon I endeavour to fhew it him in every point of view, to lead him by every path, to fpeak in fuch a manner that a fingle movement fhall not pafs but he fhall perceive it, in order that he may judge himfelf of the principle which produces it.

Did I take the refult on myfelf, and fay, Such is my character, he might think, if I would not deceive him, that I might deceive myfelf. But in particularifing with fimplicity every thing that has happened to me, all my actions, all my thoughts, all my feelings, I cannot lead him to error, unlefs I will; and even if I would, I fhould not eafily attain it in this manner. 'Tis he muft affemble the elements and determine the being they compofe; the refult muft be his work, and if he then miftakes, all the error will be his

own

own.   Now, it is not sufficient to this end that my recitals are faithful; they must be exact. It is not for me to judge of the importance of the facts; I must tell them all, and leave the care of the choice to him. I have endeavoured to do it hitherto with all my courage, and I shall not relax in what follows.   But the memory of the middle age is always weaker than that of our younger years.   I began by making the best I possibly could of these last. If the other do not come back with the same force, some impatient readers may perhaps grow tired; but for my part, I shall not be sorry for my labour. I have only one thing to fear in this undertaking; it is not saying too much, or telling falsities; but it is, not saying all, or being silent on truths.

END OF THE FOURTH BOOK, AND OF THE FIRST VOLUME.

CPSIA information can be obtained
at www.ICGtesting.com
Printed in the USA
BVHW061945030221
599247BV00008B/760